ABUNDANT
LIFE

M. SMITH

ISBN 978-1-63885-122-6 (Paperback)
ISBN 978-1-63885-123-3 (Digital)

Covenant Books, Inc.
11661 Hwy 707
Murrells Inlet, SC 29576
www.covenantbooks.com

CONTENTS

INTRODUCTION

This world has many ideas, opinions, and definitions of what abundant life is or what it should be. When I started this book, I asked several Christian and non-Christian friends of mine to define "abundant life." I actually enjoyed this question because some gave the same answers, some were dumbfounded, and some had interesting responses. Most of my non-Christian friends, for instance, would say something engaging, such as "It is having everything you want" or "It is having a lot of money." My Christian friends, on the other hand, came out with different answers, such as "It is a thankful life," "It is a life full of meaning," or "It is obeying God." These definitions are obviously true depending on the person and situation. However, abundant life in this book is not financial wealth, fame, fortune, or power, as the world defines it to be. It is not about religion, mysticism, or transcendental meditation, but it is about life that is mentally, physically, and spiritually abundant. It is living the life that was intended in the beginning. It is about life that is meaningful, full of peace, love, contentment, happiness, and joy. However, abundant life is not always perfect since it comes with challenges as well.

Tests, trials, and miseries are part of life whether we like it or not. They are bumps that jolt us out of our comfort zones that can leave uncomfortable scars. These challenging times can be painful or difficult, especially if a person does not fully understand or realize why these situations happen. But these bumps do not have to be painful; it can be full of peace, understanding, comfort, or grace. It can have positive outcomes such as endurance, understanding, peace, increased knowledge, or a better life.

Many miss out on abundant life because they are not aware or they do not know what life is or what it should be. They lack a true perspective on life. To some, life is growing up, getting married, making money, protecting families, maintaining a home, taking care of kids until they grow old and then retire. Life to some is taking care of responsibilities. But there are more to life than just responsibilities. The life that the Creator of life intended for us is to be fruitful and abundant. He intended for us to prosper and live the true life. He did not intend for us to have a miserable, burdensome, or difficult life. But even through difficult times, a person with abundant life can say, "Though I am weak, I am strong, and though I am poor, I am rich." This is the secret of abundant life.

This book will illustrate abundant life through spiritual growth, physical wellness, intellectual growth, and through relational and emotional mastery. It will illustrate how these elements could make life abundant. It will focus on right living and not wealth, money, power, or prestige. Chapter 1 will frame the foundation of the beauty of life, and chapters 2, 3, 4, 5, and 6 will demonstrate the beauty of spiritual growth through Christ. Chapters 7 and 11 touches on understanding emotions, and chapter 8 will discuss the wealth associated with physical health. Chapters 9, 10, 12, and 13 will touch on the elements that really matters in life and that we can improve and change to make life more abundant, and chapter 14 will engage in the abundance of intellectual pursuit.

This book focuses more on spiritual growth because it is the fundamental foundation of anything and everything that we do. Every element of life that will be discussed is affected by spiritual growth. Our decision-making processes, physical, intellectual, and emotional aspects of our living are positively influenced by our spiritual growth, leading to positive well-being. Spiritual growth is the wellspring of life. It is the food and water, the nourishment, if you will, of our well-being. A person's well-being is nourished not only by food but by spiritual growth as well. It is the secret power behind abundant living. Unknown to many, true riches lie not in money but in spiritual wealth.

Abundant life does not magically happen in this world. It takes training, learning, nourishing, and nurturing the spiritual, intellectual, physical, relational, and emotional elements of life. It takes effort, energy, patience, kindness, and love. It is intellectually and consciously knowing how to make correct choices and decisions that produce positive results. It is like creating a beautiful painting or a musical masterpiece; correctly building and piecing the right elements together makes it work—whole, perfect, and complete. A beautiful musical composition, for instance, works only if the notes are perfectly composed, if the lyrics touches the soul, and the singers and musicians play their parts in perfect harmony. Likewise, correctly instituting the elements of right living makes life pleasant and worth living. There are many factors to consider in order to live a life worth living; however, the essential and fundamental elements mentioned above—the spiritual, intellectual, physical, and relational growth— are I think the most important components. Spiritual growth not only nourishes our soul, but it also helps us live in peace and harmony with God, others, and ourselves. Intellectual growth helps us reach our God-given potentials. Physical growth helps us keep our body healthy, and relational growth makes us love others more than we love our selves. Abundant life could be difficult for some. But to some, abundant life is as easy as admiring the beauty of everything and anything that surrounds us.

The beautiful environment is one of the contributors of abundant life. Without mountains, trees, flowers, and animals, the earth is empty and without beauty.

CHAPTER 1

ABUNDANT LIFE IN THE BEGINNING

The Beauty of the Environment

In order to firmly grasp the elements of abundant life and to understand and fathom the actual beauty of our existence, let us first start with the environment and recognize the wealth and joy that it brings to our everyday living. Unknown to many, the creation is one of the major contributors to abundant life. Without trees, flowers, animals, fish, rivers, and mountains, the earth is devoid of beauty. However, this splendor is sometimes overlooked and undermined in spite of the beautiful essence and happiness that it brings to life.

In the beginning, the Creator lavished the
earth with beautiful living creatures, with
majestic mountains and falls to make living
on earth joyful, exciting, and fulfilling

In the beginning, the Creator lavished the earth with beautiful living creatures, with mountains and falls to make living on earth joyful, exciting, and fulfilling. The creator created this world so every living thing that lives in it will enjoy it and flourish. He made everything with care and precision and bountiful that it is more than suitable for having an abundant life. It is one of the wonders of creation that some cannot comprehend. It is awe-inspiring and magnificent. When one takes the time to admire and sincerely explore in their heart the beauty of our surrounding, one will discover the superb beauty of creation. One will find out, for instance, that the mountains and falls are majestic and the forests are breathtaking. Anyone who have seen Niagara Falls in Canada, Yosemite Park in California, and the Grand Canyon in Arizona knows the profound grandeur of creation. Everything is created perfectly, just the way it should be. The Creator created delicate butterflies, fish, deer, and birds that add magnificence to the earth. He created vegetables and fruits that are delicious and make us healthy. He made trees and flowers that are pleasing to our whole being. This beauty, excellence, and wonder is what makes earth a desirable place to be.

How many planets have we found that are as suitable for life as the Earth? There may be other planets out there; however, today, the Earth is the only planet we know that is suitable for human life. It is our gift from God (the Creator) to love, cherish, and enjoy. It is the only planet we know that has beautiful living creatures that the Creator declared, "It is good!"

The creation is impressive, but unfortunately, some do not appreciate this marvelous blessing. It is betrayed and considered ordinary, normal, common, or just a thing. To some, this beautiful environment has become like a wall of a house; it is taken for granted and unappreciated. Understandably, some do not recognize or see the beauty due to the distractions in life, where we find little time to appreciate God's creation. To some, life has been erroneously focused on surviving alone. Some have neglected to enjoy this paradise, to celebrate life, to savor living, and to appreciate the gift that was given to us. Unfortunately, many miss out on the essential significance and joy that the creation brings to life. Many are unable to comprehend that this beautiful environment is the fundamental background of the beauty of life.

I once heard a president's wife being interviewed about her beauty secret. When asked "What is one of your secrets for looking young?" she replied, "It's because I see beauty all over, because God's creation is beautiful." When one truly sees the beauty of God's creation, one cannot complain about anything.

The earth and everything in it is aesthetically created for our wonder. The millions of species of different plants and animals are numerous they could not have evolved by themselves. The numerous kinds of flowers, trees, birds, dogs, humans, are beautiful. And yes, even the ugliest person in the world is good-looking, as you will find out later. The earth is magnificent that when the Creator looked at everything, He must have sighed with a smile and said, "Aah, it is good" (Genesis 1:31).

Everything was excellent in every way. To some who appreciate and recognize this wonderful gift, they marvel at the intricate design and the delicate but artistic features of the butterfly. They take time to admire the different colors and sizes of roses and say, "Aah, it is truly beautiful." They appreciate the different trees that are stately impressive and the flowers that give color and beauty to their surroundings. Some admire the enigma and the splendor of the different kinds of animals that add joy, meaning, abundance, and beauty to their lives, whether it is a fish, cat, dog, or iguana. Some wonder at the supreme intelligence of the designer. They take time to look at the creation and acknowledge the awesomeness of God that is reflected in them. They appreciate and enjoy the abundant provision of their heavenly Father that made life wonderful and pleasing. They know that their Creator is the best designer and the best painter they will ever know. They see the beauty and profound wonder of providence that made this earth a perfect place to be.

The Profound Wonders of Creation

Understanding and learning the profound wonders of creation that is revealed in many ways are important to abundant life. Two profound wonders are important in understanding the deeper meaning and relevance of creation. First, it is important to recognize and realize that God's abundant provision was made because of His love for humanity. Second, it is also important to see and recognize His attributes in His creation; meaning, one should be able to recognize God's signature in the things that He has made.

It is important to know who the maker is so we can put things in perspective. Just like when we are looking at a painting like the *Mona Lisa*, we are as interested to know who the painter is as we are in the painting since the painting says a lot about the painter. But unfortunately, many ignore the Creator of the earth, and because of it, many fail to recognize the grand design such as God's deep love for humanity and His awesome works and attributes in His creation. Tracy Smith, a PhD student at the time of this writing, explained it well when he said,

> There is an innate awareness of God that the Creator of life embedded in humanity. Those who deny God's existence block any intrinsic awareness of God that might exist within. So, one does not see any longer the external revelation of God in the object itself. The intrinsic awareness is blocked; hence, one does not necessarily see the beauty of the butterfly that is intrinsic to the butterfly. One sees the beauty but does not see the act of creation because he or she no longer allows for the intrinsic awareness that reveals it to her or him. And so, the atheist or the agnostic suppresses the inner ability to realize that God created the hands proportionate to one another. Young kids believe easier than adults, because

adults can have a tendency to block the capacity of inner revelation obtained through the external revelation discovered in nature itself.

Many suppress the knowledge of God, and as a result they are unable to perceive the love and the revelation that is manifested in His creation. Revelation here means that by studying the details of His creation, we can develop a conclusion or inferences of God's attributes in the things He has made. We can recognize God's glory in His creation. It means that because of the intricate, mystical, and exquisite designs of His creation, we can know how awesome, intelligent, and powerful God is. When I see lightning, for instance, I see God's power. When I see rain, I see God's provision for the just and the unjust. When I see the sun, I see God's unconditional love for humanity. When I see the beautiful flower or the butterfly, I see God's love for delicate beauty. The Bible says, "The heavens declare the glory of God, and the sky proclaims the work of His hands. Day after day they pour out speech; night after night they communicate knowledge" (Psalm 19:1, 2) and "From the creation of the world His invisible attributes, that is, His eternal power and divine nature, have been clearly seen, being understood through what He has made" (Romans 1:20). One of the famous theologians in the early twentieth century, Emil Brunner, said,

> The world is the creation of God. In every creation the spirit of the creator is in some way recognizable. The artist is known by all his works... Wherever God does anything, he leaves the imprint of his nature upon what he does. Therefore, the creation of the world is at the same time a revelation, a self-communication of God.[1]

The world in itself is a revelation of God. It is God's self-communication to humanity

God's power and love is revealed in His creation. But a person who separates God from His creation is unable to see that everything is created for our joy and pleasure. Everything becomes merely a convergence of accidental events without any real purpose or reason. One may be able to enjoy the good weather or the beautiful beach, for instance, but that person does not fully comprehend the depth of the beauty and grasp the grand design. One does not fully appreciate the purpose of the good weather or the beach, and hence, he or she fails to not only thank and admire the Maker but fully experience the joy in his or her heart as well. True joy is knowing that we have an awesome God that loves us, who provides for our needs and more. True joy is thanking the Lord for providing humanity beautiful gifts, such as roses that gives color, aura, and aroma to our surroundings, the beautiful beach, or the beautiful weather that brightens our day. These wonderful gifts not only illustrate His abundant provision but communicate His great love as well. This is one of the profound wonders of creation that bring about true joy and contribute to life's abundance.

My brother and I were once sitting on his sofa staring at his seemingly enormous aquarium (since it took one-third of his living room) with beautiful, colorful fish. He commented on how beautiful the fish and how expensive some of them were. I, on the other hand, acknowledged God's awesome design in these creatures. It is awesome how they have different colors, sizes, and shapes that make the aquarium attractive and pleasurable to watch. I told my brother, "Do you know how dull this tank would be if there were only one kind of fish? Do you know how dull this world would be if there were only one kind of fish? Do you know who designed those fish and who put colors in them that makes them look magnificent? An intelligent and artistic Designer did." Many attempt to make myths and explanations as to how this could possibly be, but a Designer truly exists.

The Creator's love permeates in His creation. Most of the time I wonder if people think the way I do. I always wonder when I travel and see someone looking at the vast expanse what that person is thinking. When he looks at the grandeur of the forest, the mountains, the rivers, and the beautiful landscape, what comes to his mind? Does he appreciate the beauty and say "Aah, it is beautiful" and move on, or does he appreciate and smile and leap for joy because these beauties were made for him?

Does one recognize that the powerful and intricate design of God's creatures keeps us on our toes, makes us wonder, and keeps us always curious and baffled, thus making our life more enjoyable and interesting? When one observes the unique traits of animals, for instance, such as the strength of a tiger and the energy of a horse that could outrun humans, does one marvel in admiration how powerful they are? Both are strong and fast, but the smaller one, the tiger, can defeat the horse. Their looks are intimidating, but they remain amazing even when tamed. Both are animals, and yet it is perplexing to know that one feeds on grass and the other on meat.

As you can see, the more a person digs deeper into the grand design, the more bewildered a person will be. If a person would take the time and, with inquisitive mind, stare at the falling snow, the falling rain, or listen to the sound of the wind, that person would understand God's marvelous works in this world. These were intended to make humanity happy. Can a person make snow or rain fall like it does in specific corners of the world? If only a person would take the time and relish and examine the details of God's creation, that person would not only be amazed but would also take a deep breath of delight and say, "Aah, it is truly amazing!" The mystery of seeds, for instance, is mind-boggling. As you may know, most seeds are dried—or in another sense, dead—before they can give life again. They literally have to die before they can be planted and produce life that transforms into fruit, flowers, trees, or vegetables. Scientist maybe able to explain the process, but it is still mind-boggling. This awesome mystery can only be highly valued and enjoyed by a person who is able to see beauty through the lens of its Creator. God's love is even more visible in the beauty of variation.

The Beauty of Variation

Variation is another delightful part of creation that is oftentimes ignored or taken for granted. The Creator intended for the world to have different colors, shapes, and sizes to not only make it beautiful but to make it more interesting, pleasing and enjoyable as well. The variety adds meaning to life and living. That's why I always thank God for diversity whether it be human, animal, or plant variations. The diversity that we find in plants, for instance, is quite fascinating, especially the different fruits, flowers, and trees that are incredible.

The Creator did not only make one sort of tree, but He made countless numbers of trees, including pine trees, flowering trees, and fruit trees. In the Bible, it says, "The Lord God planted all sorts of trees in the garden—beautiful trees that produced delicious fruit" (Genesis 1:21).

The Lord God planted all sorts of trees in the garden-beautiful trees that produced delicious fruit

But most of the time, we take diversity for granted, not appreciating that variety enhances the aesthetics of the already delightful surrounding. The numerous kinds of fruits all over is one of God's creations that humanity enjoys but are underappreciated. There are so many of them, and almost all of them are delicious. And the amazing thing is that they all taste different—a banana tastes like a banana, an apple like an apple, an orange tastes like an orange, etc. The Creator made many different kinds to please our distinct taste buds. It's hard to believe, for instance, that there were thousands of varieties of apples grown in America in the 1800s. However, most of them no longer exist. We were given plenty of choices since some like green apples, some red, and I particularly like the yellow ones. There were tens of thousands distinct varieties of rice as well. I love basmati with Indian food, calrose with American dishes, and jasmine with Chinese or Filipino food. My favorite dessert is *biko*, a Filipino dessert made with sweet sticky rice, coconut, and brown sugar. It is remarkable to digest and think that we are given the privilege to see, taste, and enjoy God's awesome gift.

The numerous kinds of fruits all over is one of God's creations that humanity enjoys but are under appreciated. There are so many of them and almost all of them are delicious. And the amazing thing is that they all taste different; a banana tastes like a banana, an apple like an apple, an orange tastes like an orange, etc.

The Creator made variation even more interesting by letting different flowers, fruits, or trees grow in different climates in all corners of the world. A person could find lychee in Asia, apples in the west, papaya in Latin America, and dates in the Middle East. But the amazing thing is that these fruits do not only add beauty to our surroundings, but they also produce vitamins that are vital for daily living. They are not only nutritious, but they have different forms, making each one unique and distinct from each other;

a banana looks like a banana, an apple like an apple, and etc. And their distinct and unique features make them beautiful. One cannot say that the banana is more beautiful than the apple. Can you imagine grapes, apples, or oranges looking all like bananas? I would go bananas—it would be boring or dull. This awesome feature is extended to humanity as well.

Humanity's Aesthetic Beauty

The beauty of humanity lies within its different colors, unique traits, and beautiful features. Humanity is the pinnacle of God's creation. We have qualities and features that are unique, profound, and beautiful that all of creation pale in comparison. Most are gifted with unique intelligence that emerge as scientists, engineers, architects, doctors, theologians, painters, carpenters, philosophers, etc. Our physical features are extraordinary it is exalted above other creations. Our eyes, for instance, are so powerful they can see all the different colors in the world. They can read, cry, smile, and see however close or far it maybe. Compared to any other animal, we are the only created being that can sing, shout, whisper, laugh, and speak as many as five or more languages. Our body is in perfect symmetry that we can do anything we set our mind to do. We can climb, crawl, sit, give ourselves a bath, ride a bicycle, or do crazy things like snowboarding, skiing, or bungee jumping. How many animals do we know that can do all this? Humans are intricately made by God, and our unique features, such as the different skin pigmentation, make us even more unique.

God has blessed humans with different skin colors for beauty and diversity. Let us imagine, for instance, that there were only whites in this world and the African Americans, the Latin Americans, or the Asians did not exist. I think that it would be so boring, just like if there were only one kind of fish in the world. I once perceived all whites as to have looked the same. They did not seem to look different to me at that time. I'm sure many of you think of the Chinese the same way. I myself am happy that, in general, people do not look the same; if we do, then we would all look like penguins in the North Pole. Nevertheless, the different unique traits and different colors, such as black, white, brown, yellow (or whatever it may be), makes people more interesting, good-looking, and amazing. I think that God created variation because it is necessary for special identification, for unique distinction, for beauty, and for diversity. Our special, strange, and unusual features make everyone attractive and extraordinary. A person's nose, for instance, makes him or her distinctive, unique, unusual, but extraordinary, whether it's a big nose, small nose, high nose, flat nose, button nose, fat nose, or whatever it may be. Likewise, a person's color adds to his or her exquisite beauty. So the next time you see someone who has different skin color or features than what you have, look at them with a heart of admiration and a smile. Look at them like you are looking at the most beautiful painting in the world. We all live in a beautiful world with beautiful people; everyone is different but good-looking. Diversity makes the world a better place to be. Without variation or diversity, the world is devoid of beauty.

We live in a world where skin color should not be judged, elevated, or condemned. It is part of our unique and beautiful feature. My husband once said, "Humans are like roses. We are beautiful whether we are red, yellow, white, or pink." Each one is as special and as beautiful as anyone else. Each one is unique deserving of respect, kindness, and admiration. God created diversity for beauty and for humans to enjoy.

Humans are like roses; whether pink, red, yellow, or white, we are all beautiful

Here's a beautiful story of a world that does not regard skin color. This is a true story of Francis Njogu Mburu, a US embassy officer who worked in Kenya the day a bomb exploded at the US embassy on August 7, 1998. He said,

> For about five hours, the 42 tribes of Kenya were replaced with one big beautiful race of Kenyans. Foreigners became Kenyans too. Nationality did not matter. Black looked white and white looked black. Nobody was an American, Italian or German. We all answered the call for help. This, I believe is the way we were meant to be. I wish you could have witnessed the harmony and unification of mankind when help was in real need. On that day, in the midst of a horrendous event, I saw the true portrait of what God made us to be.[2]

Francis went on to say, "That day, skin color and language mattered less. That day, the usually greedy men who operate 'matatus'—our form of public transportation—let us ride for free. Even the rich man who usually drives alone in his spotless Mercedes Benz picked up three or four dusty, bleeding passengers and did not even care that his seats got stained." When one sees beyond a person's skin color, he or she will discover the beauty of diversity and the preciousness of humanity.

Growing up in one of the developing countries, I did not know what racism was. As a matter of fact, come to think of it, I do not even know if we have racism in our vocabulary. Anyhow, back then, we seldom saw foreigners in our city when I was a kid. But I remember how awed we children were to see someone who was tall and black or tall and white. Yes, for some reason, the foreigners were all taller than we were. We were so awed we followed them from a distance; some who were bold stayed beside the foreigners. Some tourists thought that we were following them for money, and some thought that we were probably weird and naïve, but we were following them because we were curious and at the same time amazed at their different features. We enjoyed watching them. When the foreigners smiled at us, we giggled with excitement. We thought highly of foreigners back then, especially when they gave us money. I see the same excitement and curiosity in other developing countries today as well.

If it's not yet obvious, the Creator intended for us to delight in life, to have abundant life as illustrated by the profound wonder of creation and the variety we find in nature. He loves us so much He designed a paradise for us to live in. He created the earth that's full of beauty and diversity for us to enjoy. This is truly the beauty and the depth of God's love to humanity.

In the beginning, Adam and Eve did not have to do anything but to enjoy God's company and His creation. They had it made, they enjoyed God's company, and they were able to enjoy and find pleasure in existence attributing creation to God. But as we all know, they disobeyed the Lord. Sin entered their life, and hence, their perfect world was shattered. They no longer enjoyed God's creation. Their paradise was lost. Their life started to focus on surviving, tilling the land and raising families. Sin has deformed the beauty of nature and existence.

Sin is a disease of life that everyone ignores and takes for granted, even though it continues to rob us of the good life that was intended in the beginning. But the Creator of life did not give up on humans; He still continues to reach out to us and tell us how to live a life full of meaning. He continues to tell us how to have a happy and everlasting life through Christ. We are missing out on the beauty of life if we do not understand and see that God created us to pour out His love for you and me.

I want to end this chapter with a paragraph from Saint Bonaventura, an Italian medieval Franciscan, scholastic theologian, and philosopher.

> Therefore, whoever is not enlightened by such
> great splendor in created things is blind; whoever

remains unheedful of such great outcries is deaf; whoever does not praise God in all these effects is dumb;... So open your eyes, alert the ears of your spirit, unlock your lips, and apply your heart that you may see, hear, praise, love and adore, magnify, and honor your God in every creature, lest perchance the entire universe rise against you. For because of this, the whole world shall fight against the unwise. But on the other hand, it will be a matter of glory for the wise, who can say with the prophet: For you have given me, O Lord, a delight in your doings, and in the work of your hands I shall rejoice. How great are your works, O Lord! You have made all things in wisdom; the earth is filled with your riches.[3]

When our spirit is being fed by the Holy Spirit,
it brings forth righteousness, positive traits,
accomplishments, purity, tranquility, and inward peace.

CHAPTER 2

ABUNDANT LIFE AND SPIRITUAL GROWTH

The creation is God's revelation of himself and of his love to humanity. To strengthen this love, He also provided us with his Spirit to know him more and to get closer to Him. Our body needs air, food, water, and rest in order to grow. Our spirit and soul need to be nourished as well, in order to flourish.

Our spiritual growth is vital to abundant living because it defines our whole reason for existence. Human beings consist of body, soul, and spirit whether we like to admit it or not. When our spirit is being fed by the Holy Spirit, it brings forth righteousness, positive traits, accomplishments, purity, tranquility of mind, and inward peace. The spring of life lies within this positive set of values that we experience through our spiritual growth. Without spiritual growth, a person will not have positive values or traits that he or she can use to relate to the world. We are devoid of genuine love, care, or goodness that we impart to others. It is through the spirit of God that we have peace in our hearts, that we defy anger, bitterness and live in love and care for others. It is through God's spirit that we become free of radicals that poison our spirit, body, mind, and soul. Without spiritual growth, we are cheating ourselves of genuine goodness and righteousness.

Spiritual Growth through Christ

Humans are designed by God to be spiritual beings. This is evident by our deep longing to search and worship deities such as sun, moon, Buddha, or anything that we have known or learned to be god. But God is the only one who claimed to be God and hence the only deity that's deserving of worship and praise. He is the only God who is worthy of reverence and honor because He is the only one who can genuinely change a person from a sinner to a saint and the only one who can make a life worthwhile.

Yes, living an abundant life means living a life through Christ. Living a life full of meaning, fulfillment, contentment, and joy is only possible if one has a personal relationship with Christ. Why? Because Jesus is the key to abundant life; true riches is found in the rich relationship with Christ. Through Christ, our sins are forgiven. It doesn't matter what we do or have done; the grace of God will lead us to Christ. Understand, sin is hell, but God's grace is heaven.

In the beginning, the Creator intended life to be perfect and more. He intended humans to act and live as normal beings, without sin, and to prosper as well. But many generations have come and gone, and humans have prospered, but we have lost the beauty of having a relationship with our Creator. We have sinned and have distanced ourselves from God. We have corrupted the life that was meant to be in the beginning. That's the reason why Jesus had to come to make our life count again. He came to transform our sinful lives into new and clean life—an abundant life. Cheating, lying, stealing and the like keeps us from having abundant life. He came to break the power of sin so we can live a life of abundance, to know our Creator once again, and to have a close relationship with Him.

Through our loving relationship with God, sadness will turn into joy and righteousness will reign. Through Christ, our sins are forgiven, and our life becomes real; it becomes a fulfilled life. Our life becomes interesting, challenging, and worth living because He becomes our teacher, protector, provider, avenger, healer, Redeemer, and more. He heals, and He transforms lives for the better. Christ is the sustenance—the nourishment—not only of our spiritual growth but of our daily living as well. He is the only one who can make our life abundant. He said, "I have come that they might have life, and that they might have it more abundantly" (John 10:10). Richard Ritenbaugh understood this verse when he explained that

> The Greek word Jesus uses in John 10:10 to describe the kind of life He came to teach His disciples is *perissón*, meaning "superabundant," "superfluous," "overflowing," "over and above a certain quantity," "a quantity so abundant as to be considerably more than what one would expect or anticipate." In short, He promises us a life far better than we could ever envision, reminiscent of I Corinthians 2:9, "Eye has not seen, nor ear heard, nor have entered into the heart of man the things which God has prepared for those who love Him" (see Isaiah 64:4). Paul informs us that God "is able to do exceedingly abundantly above all that we ask or think" (Ephesians 3:20).[4]

Life with Christ is full of blessings, it is beyond our expectations; it is good, it is precious, it is secure, and it is stable. On the other hand, life without Jesus is no life; it is unstable, unsecured, and uncertain, which will be illustrated further later. But having a personal relationship with Jesus is safe and secure because He is the Shepherd that lovingly protects His sheep.

In Proverbs 2:8, it says, "He guards the paths of justice and protects those who are faithful to Him." In Psalms 9:9–10, it reads, "The Lord is a shelter for the oppressed, a refuge in times of trouble. Those who know your name trust in you, for you, O Lord have never abandoned anyone who searches for you." And in the beautiful Psalm 23, it also states, "Even when I walk through the dark valley of death, I will not be afraid, for you are close beside me. Your rod and your staff protect and comfort me." Our life becomes certain in the loving hands of Christ who guides us every day, who makes sure that our well-being is taken care of, and who keeps us from harm. Our life becomes precious because it is under the protection of an awesome Father who created the earth and who is an all-powerful God. Under Jesus's protection one can experience the best of life here on earth in preparation for heaven.

Life is abundant through Jesus because not only will He protect us from harm but He will also reveal to us true life. Jesus said, "I am the way, the truth, and the life" (John 14:6). This is a deep theological statement. However, "I am the way" means that God loves us so much that He sent His Son to die for our sins, and through Jesus's death, we are redeemed from hell here on earth and in heaven someday. Jesus took the punishment that was meant for us because of our sinfulness. Hence, because He redeemed us, we are certain that when we die, we will go to heaven. He becomes the only "way" to heaven. But one might say, "Jesus did not have to die for my sins. I can take the punishment myself." I say no, you can't because your sin is too great that no punishment nor sacrifice is enough, not even if you offer a thousand sacrifices. As we progress through this book, you will see that sin is a serious crime deserving of serious punishment.

Jesus is "the life" because if we ask God to forgive our sins and be willing not to sin anymore and then believe in what Jesus has done for us on the cross (He died for your sins), and through prayer, we invite Jesus to come into our life and make Him our personal Savior, then the most awesome thing will happen—His spirit will come to us. He will come into our hearts and make all things new. And if the Holy Spirit enters our life, we are born again. We have a new life because the bad spirit's power is now broken, and the good spirit, the Holy Spirit, now has power to guide our spirit if we allow the Spirit to do so. Everything from then on will change. We are not the same anymore; we have a brand-new system that is instilled in us that will make our life better. The Holy Spirit will create a clean heart in us and a new life just like what Paul, the writer of Corinthians, described long ago. He said,

"Therefore if anyone is in Christ, he is a new creation; old things have passed away; behold all things have become new" (2 Corinthians 5:17) and "He has changed us to a new person, so that we can do the good things He planned for us long ago" (Ephesians 2:10). But again we have to remember that this life-changing process is only possible if we allow the Holy Spirit to guide our life. "All this newness of life is from God, who brought us back to himself through what Christ did. For God made Christ, who never sinned to be the offering for our sin, so that we could be made right with God through Christ" (2 Corinthians 5:18, 21). Because of Christ and our faith in Him, we can now come fearlessly into God's presence, assured of his glad welcome (Ephesians 3:12). Jesus is "the life" because He came so that we can live a life that's free from the power of sin.

Jesus is "the way" because now we can come to God, and He opens His arms of welcome to us if we accept God's offering—His Son as an offering for our sins. He is "the truth" because now that we have accepted Christ as our Lord and Savior, we have the Holy Spirit within us to reveal the truth, to reveal the things of God, and to teach us the reality of right living. He is the truth because anything that goes against His prescription of right living could hurt us. Cheating, for instance, goes against the God given way of life; it messes our life up.

God is the only one who can tell us how to live the true life because He created life. He is in the business of giving life. He created the world, He gave life to the world, and He gave His life for the world. He is the only transcendent deity who has power and who can fill our life with blessings. He has the answers to the questions "Why me, Lord?" or "Why am I in this world?" This world is full of advice claiming to have the things that will fill our lives with happiness, but don't give credit to most of what the world tells you. The truth is that most of the solutions they offer is short-lived and fleeting. Life through Jesus is abundant; it is real, it has meaning, purpose, power, and has many blessings, and it is eternal.

Why Christ?

Now a person might ask, "Why in the world would I need Jesus to have an abundant life? Surely, I can do it on my own." I say, no, you can't because without Christ, life is a failure; apart from God are sin and evil things. We need Jesus to make everything right. That is why God sent His Son, Jesus, to give us life. The Bible says it, "Whoever has the son has life; whoever does not have the son does not have life" (1 John 5:12). Do not be deceived—a person cannot do it on his own. Apart from God, you can do nothing, and living a life without Christ is living in darkness, which I will explain later. The key to abundant life is losing ourselves to Christ. He offers a life full of peace, love, and righteousness. Through Christ we will lack nothing because He will supply all our need (Philippians 4:19). Christians look and depend on Christ for right living because He offers real, authentic, and just living. To the dead, He gives life. To those who are lost, He is the way, the door, and the shepherd. To those who do not know the truth, He is the truth. To those who are hopeless, He is the hope. To those who are hungry, He is the bread of life. And to those who are in darkness, He is the light.

By just being good or by doing it on your own, you will miss out on the real purpose of life. Without Christ in your life, you are like a child without a parent who grows up without love and direction. You do not have a good spirit that empowers you to become a better you. You are like a person in a boat without a captain, not knowing how to navigate the sea. Without Christ, you are like sheep without a shepherd. Sheep do not have a sense of direction; they usually get lost, and they do not know where to go. That's the reason why they need a shepherd to lead them home, to bring them to the water or to the pasture. Through Christ, our life will have a sense of direction. Through Christ, our life becomes right and genuine, just like a genuine diamond or an authentic gold. When we buy things like gold, diamond, leather, silk, or antiques, we usually want the real ones. We should also desire the real life that was intended in the beginning. Christ desires that we change from the inside out. He desires that we change not just to live a "good life" or to please others but to genuinely change to please ourselves and our Creator.

We need Christ to take our being deeper than we could ever do. He can do this because Christ is in you (Colossians 1:27). Christ moves our lives to the positive; he removes the negative and infuses us with positives. He makes the ordinary extraordinary. He removes darkness and turns it into light. He helps remove the sin in our lives and changes it to something better if we only allow Him to do so. He can turn a nobody into somebody. He can turn a shepherd into a king and a murderer into a redeemer of life. He gives us the tools to overcome sin, evil, or temptation. I once heard a testimony of a famous country singer who used to live in promiscuity, sex, drugs, and alcohol and whose life has changed for the better. He said, "When I decided to follow Christ, I thought that He would take away my love for music but, I was thankful that He did not. Instead, He inspired me to sing love songs and family songs."

Life through Jesus has power; He gives us the power and strength to do the right things. The Bible says it, "By His mighty power at work within us, he is able to accomplish infinitely more than we would even dare to ask or hope" (Ephesians 3:20). With Christ all things are possible (Matthew 19:26). He empowers us to go through struggles, trials, and temptations. In these times, He is always by our side, enabling and encouraging us like a cheerleader yelling, "You can do it! I know you can do it!" and "Yeah!" when we are triumphant. He empowers us to live a life of fulfillment and not disappointment. God's power within us makes positive contributions to self, others, and the world.

"By His mighty power at work within us, he is able to accomplish infinitely more than we would even dare to ask or hope" (Ephesians 3:20).

Christ is in the business of changing lives for the better. I used to work in a manufacturing company where 95 percent of the workforce were men. Some of them liked to show off their manliness by being big and loud and by bragging about their womanizing and clubbing experiences. I met one of them several years after I left the company. He was still big, bold, and loud, but this time, instead of bragging about women, he was bragging about Christ. He said, "My wife and children left me a year ago, but luckily for me I found Christ. He has changed my life tremendously. I am trying to get my family back together, it may take some time, but for now, my focus is on Christ." I have never seen him again, but I have no doubt in my heart that his wife and children welcomed him back because God is in the business of building families and lives. He does not destroy them. When we allow God to take control of our lives, he gives us the will and the power to do the right things. We have His spirit, His word, and His grace to overcome the world.

But for us to attain real life, we should also have a genuine heart for God, and not just for show, make-believe, or pretentious. There is a big difference between a religious person and a person who is after God's own heart. There is a difference between a person who believes and a person who truly believes and obeys. Satan believed God, for instance, but he also disobeyed; he did not want to follow God. In the Bible, there is a difference between David and Saul, and Joseph and his brothers. David and Joseph truly believed and obeyed God regardless of their circumstances. Saul and Joseph's brothers, on the other hand, believed in God as well, but they did not have the genuine love for God that David and Joseph had. As a result, God blessed both Joseph and David and made them rule kingdoms.

What does it take to have a genuine heart for God, you may ask. The answer could be debatable, but my answer would be clear conscience, obedience, unwavering love, and faith—trusting dependence on God alone. Most of the great men in the Bible, like Joseph and David, were utterly dependent on God. Joseph maintained a clear conscience by forgiving his brothers. He demonstrated his obedience and unwavering love to the Lord by avoiding sin, as evident by running from his master's wife's enticements. David, on the other hand, loved God so deeply that he was after God's own heart. He knew God so well that God was his Savior, Friend, Father, and Boss. He became totally dependent on God. Hence, a genuine heart is demonstrated in a genuine faith without hypocrisy. A genuine heart lives purely on the reliance of God's will. It is a true, sincere, undisguised, faithful, and obedient heart.

Paul, in the New Testament, before he became a Christian, believed in God as well. But not until God revealed himself to him did his heart became on fire for Christ. Christ changed Paul's life—from a Christian persecutor and a murderer to a preacher and redeemer of life. Christ always changes people for good and never worse, even better to those whose hearts genuinely long for Him. Some people believe in deities, but they do not even know if what they believe in is real or genuine. Who but Christ offers genuine, righteous, and eternal life?

Eternal Life

Yes, it is also worth mentioning that living a life through Christ is not only abundant but also eternal. Jesus said, "I am the resurrection and the life. He who believes in me will never die (John 11:25). Jesus gave his life to restore us to eternal life. However, most people nowadays ignore the fact that there is second life, and what's more, they do not want or even care about eternal life. Why? because they have been living a life of sin and hopelessness. Their life and expectation are focused on this lifetime alone. They have never experienced the real life that is full of love and peace. Some have lived in misery, pain, and suffering. Some have been bored and unproductive because they explored unintelligent things like mysticism or occult. To some, life is too burdensome, and hence, they do not care about the afterlife. Some did not want this life in the first place, why would they even bother with another life? They are tired of living this life, why would they be encouraged with eternal life? One should not suffer from carrying this heavy load or from living in darkness. Through Christ, there is hope for heaven here on earth and through eternity. Through Christ, the hope of eternal life starts here on earth because "Christ in you is the hope of glory" (Colossians 1:27). Living eternal life in heaven is the hope that Christians have for a perfect life.

In fact, Christians were promised that the afterlife is better than the life we have here on earth. And unlike other belief systems that believe that you will become a fox or a squirrel when you die, through Christ, eternal life is in heaven.

In heaven, there will be no more tears, no more sorrow, no more pain and suffering, no more hunger, and no more death. A person will no longer be subject to injury; righteousness will reign, and everything will be wonderful.

Can you picture yourself in heaven someday? If not, here are other pictures of life that is not just about getting through life. This is a picture of hope where humans and animals no longer kill each other for survival.

> The wolf shall live with the lamb,
> the leopard shall lie down with the kid,
> the calf and the lion and the fatling together,
> and a little child shall lead them.
> The cow and the bear shall graze,
> their young shall lie down together;
> and the lion shall eat straw like the ox.
> The nursing child shall play over the hole of the asp,
> and the weaned child shall put its hand on the adders' den.
> They will not hurt or destroy on all my holy mountain; for the earth will be full of the knowledge of the Lord as the waters cover the sea. (Isaiah 11:6–9)

The best picture in the world that you'll probably ever see is a child playing and leading a tiger, lion, fox, or a snake on a green grass to home. This picture is what heaven is. In addition, in heaven, we will be living with God and His angels. We will be living in mansions as God's children. If one studies the awesomeness of heaven and what it is like, then one could not help but be inspired and be excited about going to heaven. One would look forward and would do anything to be in heaven someday.

I cannot describe heaven the way it really is, but assume for a moment that heaven is like an island paradise. It is like the island in the *Blue Lagoon* movie a long time ago. Imagine for a moment that you are living in this beautiful island. This paradise is magnificent; it is breathtaking. This majestic kingdom is full of exquisite fruits, fish, animals, and vegetation. Everything is fresh; the water is pure, and the vegetables and fruits grow and ripe naturally. The animals are friendly and harmless. The lion plays with the children, and the cobra dances with the wind. The ape brings ripe fruits and fresh coconuts, and the birds bring you nuts and berries. The weather is always perfect, with occasional showers but certainly no hurricanes or tornadoes. The birds and fish are domesticated they can be fed with hands, but they freely fly in the sky or swim in the vast sea. It is definitely a stress-free life—no bills to pay, no house payment to be worried about, and no insurance or car payment to think about. Time becomes irrelevant for you can go to sleep when you are tired and wake up whenever you are rested. It is always sunny, calm, peaceful, and full of tranquility.

Now compare this serene and restful atmosphere to a horrible jungle like perhaps the lost streets of New York, for instance, where people could rob you and a gun could be pointed at your head if you took the wrong turn. The banker, the lawyers, and the insurance companies are after your money, and your neighbor is constantly complaining about your dog. Stress is an everyday struggle caused by bills and unsecured jobs. Your boss is overly demanding, and the police are continually knocking at your door. People are like the weather—they are unpredictable, unfriendly, and could be harmful. You could be living in an awful jungle!

Isn't living in paradise far more attractive than living in a city that wants to kill your body and soul? Isn't living in quietness and tranquility with fresh air better than living in a place where noise and chaos abound and the air is polluted? Heaven starts here on earth if we are in Christ, but without Christ, life is hopelessness.

Life without Christ

Let me demonstrate further a life without Christ. As mentioned earlier, life without Christ is a life in sin. Without Christ, life is empty, and it is always searching for the meaning of life. It is full of wrongdoing, hatred, anger, and the like. People without God like to say curse words, and they are angry with everything and in anything, whether it's the world they live in, their co-worker, their neighbor, their president, or the pizza delivery boy who was late and sweaty because he could not find the place and could probably lose his job because of it. These people like to kill, steal, cheat, and lie. Most, if not all, agree with aborting babies and taking the lives of old people or the terminally ill. They pretend to live moral lives, but their so-called morality is only skin deep. They would, for instance, rally against death penalty, but they favor abortion. They would rather allow for the criminal to live and kill the innocent. They claim to believe in God, but they deny Him by the way they live (Titus 1:16). They will even go to church, but when they go home, go to work or to a party, they use the name of the Lord God in vain. Some do not respect their mother, father, brothers, or sisters, or anyone, not even their president or their God. "Their god is their appetite, they brag about shameful things, and all they think about is this life here on earth" (Philippians 3:19). Some of them do not believe in absolute truth, they claim that there is no truth, that truth is relative. They do not believe that the Bible is the Word of God, and they claim that it's just a book, even though the Bible has stood the test of time, and it's the only best-selling book with billions of copies sold all over the world. Moreover, they do not believe that God exists because they either see the evil in this world and question why God allowed such a thing or they have not encountered God personally. They usually question and blame God for everything, but they never appreciate what God has done or provided for them. There is always a void in their life; there is always something missing that they will never understand or fill. If they had understood, then they would know that only God could fill that void. Now you might think that all of the above are harsh, untrue, and perhaps not you. But allow me to illustrate further a life without God in a simpler way.

If you are living without God, you easily sin, and you do not even know it. Allow me to show you how. The first thing that comes to mind is lying (not telling the truth). Now we all know that lying is a sin. It is one of the "thou shall nots" in the Bible (Exodus 20:16).

If the Holy Spirit is not living in you, or if God is not your God, then lying comes easily. For instance, if someone calls you through the phone and you do not want to talk to that person, you easily whisper to the person who answered the phone, "Tell him/her I'm not here." But the truth is you were there, and what's worse, you just taught the person who answered the phone (no doubt your kid or your husband) how to lie. Another illustration is when you just don't want to go to work that day or perhaps you woke up late, you then call up your boss and say, "I am not feeling well," even though you are feeling fine but you just woke up late. You see, lying comes easy, but to the godly, these petty lies are serious sins. The godly knows that if you lie on little things, you will also lie on big things; you would easily lie to your husband, children, boss, to the judge, or to the government. Lying is sin because it is used to deceive or to cover up a corruption. It is the devil's tool to corrupt a person, giving way to deceitful hearts.

Stealing is another illustration. I used to walk out of the doctor's office with a pen that I had just borrowed and not feel guilty about it. I would happily keep the pen instead so I wouldn't have to spend money on buying pens. I also used to walk out of the store with more money because the cashier made a mistake and gave me extra change. I used to steal money from my mother when I was in high school and felt guilty about it, but I spent the money anyway. However, when I became a Christian, I became aware of stealing. I am now mindful every time I take a pen. I would always take it back even if I had to return it on my next doctor's visit. Stealing is a sin no matter how you package it, whether it's simply a pen or receiving extra money from the cashier. You might say, "Well, it's no big deal. It's just a pen." But do you even wonder why your doctor or even the banks have now tied up their pens to their clipboards or to their tables? Yes, it is a big deal! Every time you steal, even if it's just petty things, you are breaking one of Gods commandments, "Thou shalt not steal (Exodus 20:15)." Eve believed in Satan's little lie, and the perfect paradise was taken away from them. What's more, their abundant relationship with God was severed. This little lie cost them their paradise. Even the soap operas on television think it's a big deal. They oftentimes show friends or a couple separating because of a little lie. And like lying, if you steal little things, what's stopping you from stealing big things?

You see, sins like lying, and stealing robs you and the person around you from having an abundant life. Not giving the extra money to the cashier could cause her to lose her job. But more importantly, you are cheating yourself from having a meaningful life. If you do not feel guilty about taking the pen from the doctor's office or saying petty lies, then you are in big trouble because you have been deceived and have been robbed of goodness. You are deceived and cheated of the righteousness that makes life abundant. The deceiver has made you believe that these sins are normal and do not hurt anyone. In fact, it is hurting you, and the people around you. It is hurting you because your credibility is questioned, and you are in danger of becoming unreliable. It is hurting the person around you because you have now taught them how to steal and lie. A person who sins, who steals, lies, and cheats, are underdeveloped, unenlightened, uncivilized, and uncultured. Sin puts you deeper and deeper in the pit. It is lawlessness, and this means that your life is going bad instead of getting better. It means that the standard of your life has become low. Yes, your standard has become low because you now have to cheat, lie, and steal just to live. Your good life is messed up because you have been controlled by the deceiver and by your sinful nature.

You see, sin is not only lawlessness but a separation from God as well. Every time you steal, cheat, and lie, you are separating yourself from God who is right and good and allying yourself with Satan the great deceiver.

But there is hope because Jesus's arms are open wide for us, even though He sees the garbage that we have piled up. He is inviting anyone—offering a better life. Christ wants to cleanse us from this garbage (sin). The reason we are not enjoying life is because we are full of dirt, we cheat, we lie, we are bitter, and we are angry with anyone who do us wrong. Unfortunately, we cannot clean ourselves for this dirt is deep within. We must allow Jesus to come into our life so we can get rid of this dirt, so we can live righteously through Him. In 1 John 4:9, it says that "God showed his love for us by sending His only begotten son into the world, that we might live through Him." Our spirits are dead, and we are in darkness because of our sinful nature. But through Jesus, we are able to live and live in the light through His Holy Spirit. Through Jesus, we can conquer and rise above the garbage and walk away into a cleaner life. Through Jesus, our lives improve tremendously, and it becomes profoundly meaningful.

But if we allow the evil spirit to rule our life, then we are doomed. Yes, believe it or not, evil spirits are real. They are very real because they are destroying our lives like a cancer or virus does to our bodies. In my opinion, we only have two choices, either we let the evil spirit or let the Holy Spirit rule our lives. By choosing the evil one, we are choosing darkness—we are lost, doomed, and destroyed. But if we choose a life through Christ, then we will live in the light with peace, hope, love, care, and righteousness. Jesus said, "I am the light of the world. If you follow me, you won't be stumbling through the darkness, because you will have the light that leads to life" (John 8:12).

Growing spiritually through Christ is what makes life abundant; because unlike other deities, Christ is active in our life. Like a loving Shepherd, He is involved in our daily living by guiding us to the right path of right living. He is for you, with you, and in you. Life through Christ is abundant because He nourishes us with truth, love, kindness, and righteousness.

CHAPTER 3

DOES GOD REALLY EXIST?

Because of living in darkness for so long and suppressing one's knowledge of God, many doubt about God's existence. They usually ask questions such as, "Is God for real?" or "Does God really exist?" My answer is yes, He is real and He exists. If you are one of those who doubt about God's existence, I challenge you to look around. Who made all this? Who made the banana, the apple, or the strawberry that you eat? Who designed the flowers, the birds, and the trees? Who made the cat or the dog that you see? Someone created it; someone designed it and made it look like a cat or a dog. Just like a house or a computer cannot just appear on its own, someone designed and build them. Just because you do not see the Creator, that doesn't mean the Creator does not exist. God exists. He revealed Himself in history, in nature, and in individual's lives every day.

God did not only reveal Himself in creation but in history as well. He revealed Himself to the world that He created, and as a result the Bible was written. He showed himself to us both ways in order for us to not have an excuse in believing Him. But not only did He reveal himself in His creation and in history, but He also reveals Himself every day to any individual who calls on Him. I am not a theologian nor a philosopher, but I will do my best to prove to you that He is real and He exists through my personal encounter and my husband's personal experience as well. First let me illustrate to you that He is real through His active involvement in my life.

God revealed Himself into my life when I decided to make Him my Lord, my Savior, my Friend, and my Father. However, even though I made this decision, I was still self-righteous; meaning, I would always believe that I am not a sinner, and I often told my husband that I am good and I don't sin. I told him I didn't kill anyone, I did not commit adultery, I did not steal, I don't lie (even though I stole and I lied), etc. So one day, while I was in the kitchen doing house chores and listening to the song "Amazing Grace" at the same time, the Lord suddenly revealed in front of me a list of my sins. My sins were so heavy and detestable I could not help but kneel and cry to God for forgiveness. After I asked for God's forgiveness, I felt light, happy, free, and forgiven. I was overcome with joy that I was crying and laughing. I could not explain how God did what He did, but it was a miracle. That day I was just doing housework oblivious to what God was about to do. But that day, He redeemed me from my sins, and from then on, my life has changed and is continually changing.

Since then, I see God's hand working in my life. Since then, there are many things that God does for me that I could not have done on my own. Since then, He provided a job for me when it was impossible for me to find one. He cured me from my sickness, and He comforted me when I need consolation. No one can comfort me like God could because He removes my worries or soothes my feeling whenever I feel that things are too rough. He would always lighten my load whenever I cry for help. Yes, God is alive, and He is active in my life. I am no longer self-righteous, but now I admit every day that I am a sinner in need of God's grace and forgiveness. I used to steal, but now whenever I walk out of the doctor's office with a pen, the Holy Spirit tells me what I've done. Every time I tell a lie, God would make sure that I am aware that I told a lie, and I would then have to fix it.

For example, I told a lie to my sister once. She was going to reimburse me half of my brother's airfare to come to Texas from New York many years ago. I told her it cost me a hundred dollars even though the total cost was only fifty dollars (I used my frequent flyer mileage, so I only had to pay for the processing fee). You see, I doubled the cost so she would pay for the entire processing fee instead of splitting the cost with me. I thought, since I was using my mileage, then she should pay for the entire fee. Come to think of it, I was not even desperate for money at that time. But right after I told her the amount, I felt very guilty that I could not bear the feeling of guilt. It was difficult for me to call and admit to her that I lied, but I had to since the lie stayed heavy in my heart. I was even afraid to pick up the phone because I thought that she would just bark at me or tell me that she will never trust me again, or worse, I thought that our relationship would be severed forever. But I called her anyway and apologized for lying and that she would have to give me twenty-five dollars only. She laughed and said, "Don't worry I will give you fifty." After I apologized, it felt like a burden was lifted off my back. I could have chosen to not apologize and move on with my life, but I chose to obey, and it felt good. Moreover, not only did it felt good, but my sister also gave me fifty, and I feel that she trusted me more, and our relationship became stronger since then. God exists, and He is watching over me, making sure that I do the right thing, making sure that my life is not going down the drain, and making sure that I keep the path to abundant life.

Now my husband, on the other hand, had encountered the Lord when he was a teenager. Before the encounter, my husband used to sell drugs and was an addict as well. His life was so messed up one day he contemplated suicide. He had a knife in his hand, but for some reason, he had some sanity left in him to decide to pray. He simply said, "God, if you are real, change my life." After this prayer, he felt that the guilt and burden of sin was lifted off him. He felt peace within him he fell asleep peacefully. The next morning, for some reason that he could not explain, he had an insatiable desire to read the Bible. He read the entire Bible during the summer. It changed his life overnight that he started pushing God to his friends who were pushers, dealers, and addicts. Because of finding the real life, instead of selling drugs, he was selling God. My husband, through God's grace, became a successful computer engineer and is now pursuing graduate degrees in philosophy and theology. God is in the business of making lives more abundant. He truly changed my husband and me. He is real, He exists, and He is active in our lives every day.

There are many Christian testimonies that are worth mentioning in this book. Most, if not all, will tell you that their life changed for the better. Those whose lives have changed would tell you that God is alive, is real, and is active in their everyday lives. I heard many testimonies from drug addicts, alcoholics, prisoners, broken families, and the like, and every one of them, including my husband and I, will tell you that because of God's love, we were snatched out of hell. I challenge you to ask a true Christian some time about their life-changing experience. I mean a true Christian, since many claim to be Christians but are not real. They are wolves in sheep's clothing. But ask a genuine Christian whose life was changed because of his or her personal encounter with the Lord.

What about Evolution?

Now many claim that God is not real because we were taught and continue to be taught that we evolved and not created. My thinking was, how did we evolve from an ape when the ape dies an ape? People living a hundred years die exactly like a person. Not a tiny tail or extra body part grew out of a person. A person grows old and the skin wrinkles, but it is still a person. If people evolved, then we should not look like a person by now; we should have continued to evolve. Our bodies should have evolved at least a tiny bit into something. In the biblical times, a person lived for a thousand years, but their physical features never changed; they got old and wrinkled, but their features are never altered or transformed.

Even scientists cannot prove that we evolved. They cannot show the missing link between human and apes. Every time they claim to have come out with something, it is always a sham. Evolutionists claim that we evolved because some of God's creation evolves. But when God created us, He created human beings, not apes. When He created apes, it stayed an ape until now. When He created the dog, it stayed a dog until now. It may have changed its color, size, or height because of crossbreeding, but it is still a dog.

How is it that most animals including humans are male or female? That could not have happened accidentally. God designed it that way so we can procreate, so we can enjoy intimate relations with our spouse. How is it that we have perfect bodies with two hands, two eyes, two feet, etc., and these parts work perfectly that it enables us to do anything we want to accomplish? The feet, for instance, are made in such a way that we are able to stand, bend, walk, dance, or run as fast as we can without falling on our face. Our hands are perfectly designed so we can gently hold on to a baby, carry heavy loads, or handle delicate things, such as splice DNA or build spaceships. What's fascinating is that all of our body parts are usable—the tongue tastes, our hands write, our nose smells, and the ear hears. No body parts are useless. These body parts could not have evolved by themselves. It is obviously made by an intelligent designer. How is it that we are not like the animals, but we are gifted with brains that could create things like buildings, automobiles, musical masterpieces, and beautiful paintings? I tell you why. Because we are truly made in the image of God. An ape until now has not built a single home. A bird has been building nests since the beginning, and the nest still looks like a nest. But humans have prospered from a shack to a mansion with an elevator. We are especially designed by the Creator of this universe, and we are immensely superior to animals with a greater capacity for engineering robots, high-rise buildings, and spaceships. Brunner once said about the image of God:

> It signifies above all the superiority of man within creation… This superior position in the whole of creation, which man still has, is based on his special relation to God, i.e. on the fact that God has created him for a special purpose-to bear his image… Man has an immeasurable advantage over all creatures.[5]

To bear God's image is an honor and an immeasurable advantage. It elevates and blesses humans with immense value and superiority over all creation. In Genesis 1:26, it says, "Then God said, Let Us make man in Our image, according to our likeness; let them have dominion over the fish of the sea, over the birds of the air, and over the cattle, over all the earth and over every creeping thing that creeps on the earth." Since we are created in the image of God, we also like to create things. Apes do not think like humans, and they cannot create or solve problems. They just sit in the jungle and chase each other. And oh yeah, they are still apes until today, and they haven't evolved a bit. As you can see, I am not a scientist, but I can see that God, in His magnificent way, created humans and animals. He created animals with distinct, unique traits. The deer, for instance, is created with keen sense to protect itself from its predators just like skunks, porcupines and dogs. But humans are God's special handiwork. We are at the heart of God's creative work; we are exquisitely and wonderfully made. David, a man who was after God's own heart, recognized this reality. In the book of Psalms, he said, "I will praise You, for I am fearfully and wonderfully made; marvelous are Your works" (Psalm 139:14).

We are not mere accidents; we are intricately designed. We are emotional, intelligent, creative, and we can fully think. We can solve difficult problems like differential calculus, and we can build airplanes, highways, and computers. We can love like crazy, and we can think and make decisions that are rational. We can cry about our loss and laugh a lot until we are embarrassed. God has gifted us with emotions so we are able to share joy and happiness, so we can empathize, love, care, or relate to others. The kind of life that the Creator bestowed to humanity is unlike any other animal. It is a special life.

But why do evolutionists always put the evolution story in the science books? It's because they do not have any credible proof to explain our existence. They do not want to accept or believe that we are created beings even though they could not rationally explain where we came from. Where did the rat, the cat, the dog, the bird, the snake, the fish, the trees, the delicious fruits, and the beautiful flowers came from? Again, there are numerous kinds of these creatures. Not only one kind but numerous.

For some of you who still need more credible facts against human evolution, there are many credible books and organizations that can prove that human evolution is a deception. Some of the popular books that I've read are *The Scientific Case Against Evolution* by Henry Morris and *The Case for a Creator* by Lee Strobel. I myself am happy that God created me. Because if I am not made by God and if I am just an accident that evolved from nothing or from an ape, then my life here on earth is meaningless—it does not have a purpose. But since I am lovingly, wonderfully, and intricately made by God, then I am happy and thankful of the opportunity to make a difference in this beautiful world that God made for me. I am special because I am made in the image of God, and I am privileged because I have the opportunity to become one of the Creator of the world's child, God's child, and to see heaven as my home someday.

Some evolutionists are not doing humanity any good by insisting on human evolution. They misrepresent God and creation because they do not believe that God created the world and everything that is in it. They want to insult or demean us by making us equal to animals. They want to make us think and feel low while, in fact, we are superior, and we have immeasurable advantage over all creation. They do not understand abundant living because they often deny the existence of God who gave us not only life but a *beautiful* life.

God showed his love for us by sending His only begotten son into the world, that we might live through Him.

CHAPTER 4

THE ENEMY OF
ABUNDANT LIVING

Knowing the enemy is crucial to abundant living because the enemy does not want you to have an abundant life. The enemy does not want you to know God, to go to heaven someday, or to enjoy life. The enemy insists that there is no God and wants you to believe that humans evolved from an ape. He is the scientist who bases his theories on deceptive facts and suppresses any alternative explanations. He is the bad spirit that tells politicians and businessmen to steal, cheat, and lie. It is the spirit that tells you that you are ugly and hopeless. It tells you that you look bad and makes you think bad. It is the spirit that tells you that happiness is having wealth and doing anything you want even though it destroys your life. It is the spirit that makes your emotion go wild and hence ruin your reputation, yourself, and your life. It is the spirit that makes a man beat his wife. It is the spirit that hardened your heart from God, closed your mind, and filled it with darkness. It teaches you not to care for right and wrong or for anyone else but yourself, and it makes you do what makes you happy even if it's wrong. It is the spirit that you do not see, but it is real, and it is ruining your life.

The enemy has many names, such as Satan, devil, demon, Lucifer, deceiver, adversary, snake, and etc. It has many appearances as well. We were always taught that the enemy is ugly and has horns and tails. But the enemy is again a deceiver—it is deceptive in appearance. Contrary to the old belief, it can actually look like an angel, a politician, a teacher, a scientist, or a celebrity. He or she can appear to be beautiful. In mafia or James Bond movies, for instance, they use beautiful women as baits or as traps to get information, to confuse, or to kill someone. The deceiver is equally the same. It could be good-looking but manipulative, corrupt, deceitful, dishonest, shady and a counterfeit. It appears to be concerned, caring, loving, real, or genuine, but in reality, it is just a façade. It prowls about like a roaring lion, seeking someone to devour (1 Peter 5:8). It hates humans, and its quest is to destroy humanity. The enemy is evil, and it is repulsive to those who know him and to those who can see the facade and deception.

The enemy distorts our decision processes; hence, it behooves us to know the enemy in order to counter his deceptions. If, for instance, we want to disrespect our parents, we need to realize quickly before it's too late that we are or were under the enemy's control. Hence, we need to either stop or apologize. Apologize for it is the right thing to do. It rebuilds broken hearts, and it heals wounds.

The spirit of the enemy is the adversary, the angel of lawlessness and of the bottomless pit. He is the ruler of this world and he is all over. He or she is in the media, at your school, in organizations, or perhaps within you. He could be teaching you the wrong way to live. The enemy is not our children though some may look, sound, or feel like one. But the enemy is the spirit of darkness that is influencing our children to make wrong decisions. Satan is the king of the dark world, and the only way to counter darkness is to expose it in the light. God is the light and the only one who can defeat darkness.

God is the light and the only one who can defeat darkness.

The following is an advice from the Bible for those who desire to defeat evil:

> Finally, my brethren, be strong in the Lord and in the power of His might. Put on the whole armor of God, that you may be able to stand against the wiles of the devil. For we do not wrestle against flesh and blood, but against principalities, against powers of wickedness in the heavenly places. Therefore, take up the whole armor of God that you may be able to withstand in the evil day, and having done all, to stand.
>
> Stand therefore, having girded your waist with truth, having put on the breastplate of righteousness, and having shod your feet with the preparation of the gospel of peace, above all, taking

the shield of faith with which you will be able to quench all the fiery darts of the wicked one. And take the helmet of salvation, and the sword of the Spirit, which is the word of God; praying always with all prayer and supplication in the Spirit, being watchful to this end with all perseverance and supplication for all the saints.

We cannot defeat evil on our own; we may think we can, but those whose hearts have not been changed by God are powerless against Satan's wiles. We need God's truth, God's word, and His spirit to conquer evil. Know the enemy because he is the enemy—he is the *destroyer of life*.

CHAPTER 5

ABUNDANT LIFE GOD'S WAY

The enemy hates and destroys lives, but Christ loves and saves them. In order to keep our lives from being destroyed, we must consider God's way of life. Christ knows all about life and living at its fullest more than anybody can ever know because He created life. His way of life is perfect; it is a noble and lofty life, elevated from the ordinary.

But in order to live an admirable life, one must first turn away from his or her sins. As mentioned earlier, sins are the garbage of life; thus, it is necessary to avoid it in order to allow God to work in our lives. He despises and abhors sin because, as mentioned earlier, it is lawlessness, and it destroys lives. It is like a poison that kills our being.

Allow me to illustrate further how sin destroys life. Alcoholism, for instance, causes abuse, neglect, sickness, and divorce. Hatred can result in killing, pain, and imprisonment. Cheating on your spouse can cause suicide, hatred, bitterness, and broken heartedness. In Proverbs 6:32, it says, "But the man who commits adultery is an utter fool for he destroys his own soul." You will read it again and again that sin is a negative element that drains and bankrupts lives. The fruit of such things is ruin and not life. That's the reason why God detests sin because it leads to death. Paul, the apostle of the Gentiles, clearly states it, "The wages of sin is death; but the gift of God is life through Jesus Christ our Lord" (Romans 6:23). Hence,

God cannot work in our lives not until we recognize that we are sinners in need of forgiveness, redemption, and salvation. We have to ask for forgiveness. "If we confess our sins, God is faithful and just and will forgive us our sins and purify us from all unrighteousness" (1 John 1:9). Without asking for God's forgiveness, His Holy Spirit will not be able to live in us. We need to make room for the Holy Spirit if we truly want an abundant life and if we want to enjoy life at its fullest.

Abundant Life with the Holy Spirit

As mentioned earlier abundant life is not about spiritualizing, but it is about right living through Jesus and through the guidance of God's love—the Holy Spirit. It is not about deep transcendental meditation, a supernatural quest, or mysticism, but it is about the Holy Spirit being active in our lives so we can let righteousness reign. It is about living under the direction of the Holy Spirit, allowing His presence to empower us to make the right decisions. Jesus said,

> If you love Me, keep My commandments. And I will pray the Father, and He will give you another Helper, that He may abide with you forever—the Spirit of truth, whom the world cannot receive, because it neither sees Him nor knows Him; but you know Him, for He dwells with you and will be in you. I will not leave you orphans; I will come to you. (John 14:15–17)

With the Holy Spirit's presence, we are empowered to make things right. The Holy Spirit helps us understand the truth and the spiritual things of God. With the Holy Spirit as our Helper, it makes living refreshing. It is like infusing good stuff into our bodies. It is a good feeling because our spirit is regenerated. Our spirit is protected from the devil's deceptions.

But one may ask, how would I know if the Holy Spirit is within me guiding or helping me? There are several things to recognize if the Holy Spirit is within you. First, you know that the Holy Spirit is present in your life if He is helping you change and He is guiding you every day. He should dominate your life and not you dominating your life. Romans 8:5,6 says that "those who are dominated by the sinful nature think about sinful things, but those who are controlled by the Holy Spirit think about things that please the Spirit." If your sinful nature controls your mind, you are not regenerated. But if the Holy Spirit controls your mind, you have been renewed. With the Holy Spirit, you lose the desire to sin or do the usual sinful habits that you usually do. You lose the desire to steal, to cheat, and lie. If you allow your fleshly desires to dominate your life, the tendency that it will lead you to trouble is high. But if you obey the Holy Spirit, it will always lead you and the people around you to a better life. The Holy Spirit is the protection from the devil.

Second, if the Holy Spirit is within you, you should be demonstrating the fruit of the Spirit. According to the Scriptures, particularly in Galatians 5:22–23, the fruit of the Spirit is love, joy, peace, longsuffering, kindness, goodness, faithfulness, gentleness, and self-control. You can't demonstrate this fruit not unless you are born again, and the Holy Spirit is active in your life. And if you have the Holy Spirit, these qualities naturally become your character. These qualities enable you to become what God wants you to become. As you may know, fruit is not made; it comes from within. The apple tree brings fruit from within. It is not made from the outside. Hence, these qualities or fruit of the Spirit come from within. Since the Holy Spirit is within you, it is able to generate impressive fruit that are not only good but are fulfilling and pleasing as well. Say, for instance, that you were used to stealing before the Holy Spirit came into your life, and now that you have the Holy Spirit, you are tempted to steal again. If, for instance, you listen to the prompting of the Holy Spirit to not steal, if you obey, the fruit of self-control will grow, and as a result you will become a better and changed person because now the sin of stealing is under your control and, at its best, gone!

Consequently, if you keep obeying the prompting of the Holy Spirit, the fruit will multiply, allowing righteousness to increase effecting holiness and godliness leading to good life.

However, one should also understand that even with the presence of the Holy Spirit in our life, our personal will power—our human spirit still exists. Our Creator will never take away the power of our free will that gives us the freedom to make decisions. But not unless we turn this power over to the guidance of the Holy Spirit can we start to encounter the life that is fully and completely God's. "For if you live according to the flesh, you are going to die. But if by the Spirit you put to death the deeds of the body, you will live. All those led by God's Spirit are God's sons" (Romans 8:13–14).

But one could also argue that the Holy Spirit is not needed since one's effort to control oneself is sufficient. A person is able to do the right things on his own. But as I have already demonstrated, it is not authentic, it is not real, it is a self-effort, and it does not have a meaning; it is just for show and will not last. But through the Holy Spirit, one can have genuine and authentic change. One's effort of good works does not genuinely bring fruit of the Spirit, but the work of the Holy Spirit does. To illustrate, if a person is visiting a neighbor who is in the hospital, and he is doing this because of duty or he has to be nice or it's because it's his neighbor or it's because he's just returning a favor, then his act is not genuine; it is a self-effort. But if he is visiting his neighbor out of compassion, love, kindness and goodness, and he even goes to the extra mile to go to the flower shop and or to the bakeshop and picks the best items for his neighbor, then this act is genuine love. He even looks forward to visiting his neighbor and it is a joy and privilege to do it. These genuine acts come naturally from God's children because this is what our Father expects of his children to act in heaven.

If we have to live in heaven or in the house of God someday, we have to act and become like His children here on earth. And if we are living in the guidance of the Holy Spirit, we are true children of God. In Romans 8:14, it says, "For all who are led by the Spirit of God are children of God… For his Holy Spirit speaks to us deep in our hearts and tells us that we are God's children" (v. 16).

Living a life through the Holy Spirit is vital because the key to understanding God is through the Holy Spirit. The Holy Spirit is the link between man and God. The Holy Spirit preserves or seals our adoption in Christ. God communicates and demonstrates His power through the Holy Spirit. Moreover, the Holy Spirit shows us the deep secrets of God so we can know the wonderful things of God. In the Bible, it says, "When He, the Spirit of truth, has come, He will guide you into all truth" (John 16:13). He is the revealer of truth. But those who are not born of the Holy Spirit cannot understand the truth from God; it all sounds foolish to them. But those who walk with the Spirit lives a life of peace and assurance because they have the Holy Spirit to reveal the truth and to guide them through life. Hence, among other things, value the Holy Spirit's presence in your life.

Abundant Life Is Obedience

Obedience comes easily when the Holy Spirit is within us. But to some, obedience is another character trait that is oftentimes difficult to do. Nowadays, many have problems obeying authority. Obedience to our parents, for instance, is sometimes burdensome since we want to do things our way, and we usually think that we know better than they do. But in fact, more often than not, they are actually correct, and they are smarter than we perceive them to be since they are older and more experienced. But it is a fact that we are all under authority whether to our parents, to our manager at work, or to God. Even the president of America has authority above him. Nevertheless, obedience to the legitimate authority is the right thing to do; it may not always be right, but under normal circumstances, obeying makes us a better person.

Obeying our parents, for instance, more often than not, leads to a successful life. I myself did not give much attention to my parents' advice to concentrate on finishing school. My parents, like most parents, kept telling us to concentrate on education because having a degree will lead to a better life. I did not listen, and consequently, I did not finish my business degree. My sister, on the other hand, finished her accounting degree. Now she is able to stand on her own. She bought a house, a car, living without depending on anyone. I, on the other hand, cannot stand on my own without relying on my husband for provision. Some people like me usually regret not obeying and suffer the consequences in the later life. I finally got my degree but at a later age. Regardless, obeying results to improved and better life, but this I know that obedience to God leads to abundant life.

In Luke 5, we read that after fishing all night, Peter and the other men were washing their nets since they had fished all night but did not catch any. Jesus got on the boat and started preaching. After preaching, He told Peter to cast his net into the deep. But Peter was reluctant to obey since they had fished all night and had caught nothing. But he said, "'Nevertheless at Your word I will let down the net.' And when they had done this, they caught a great number of fish, and their net was breaking. So they signaled to their partners in the other boat to come and help them. And they came and filled both boats, so that they began to sink." If you want a boatload of blessings, you should obey God.

Obedience to God bring about admirable and honorable life as well. For it is in surrendering oneself to God that we conquer evil. It is in obedience to God that we are able to gain wisdom, knowledge, and live righteously. It is when we obey God that we experience the joy that surpasses human understanding. It is a joy that is full of gladness, delight, satisfaction, and fulfillment. One cannot lose by being obedient to God. When a Christian man named Jomich, for instance, is prompted by God to do something good for his poor neighbor—whether it is helping them find a job, buying them some food, or sending one of the children to school—his act of obedience will not only bring about admirable deeds and satisfaction but joy and honor as well. Just like if I had obeyed my parents' advice to finish school, my life could have been more admirable and satisfying. In the Bible, God said lovingly, "My child, don't lose sight of good planning and insight. Hang on to them, for they fill you with life and bring you honor and respect."

But the outcome of obeying God does not only produce blessings and nobility but also brings us closer to God. That's why the godly likes to obey because they know too well that His commandments emit life and love, and it brings them closer to the Lord, just like when we are obedient to our parents. Jesus said, "He who has My commandments and keeps them, he it is who loves Me; and he who loves Me shall be loved by My Father, and I will love him, and will disclose Myself to him" (John 14:21).

Moreover, the godly naturally obeys because they know that obedience brings a long and satisfying life. In Proverbs 3, God instructs us to keep in our minds and heart His words: "My child, never forget the things I have taught you. Store my commands in your heart, for they will give you a long and satisfying life." In the next chapter, He also says, "Pay attention, my child, to what I say. Listen carefully. Don't lose sight of my words. Let them penetrate deep within your heart, for they bring life and radiant health to anyone who discovers their meaning."

Understandably, to some it takes courage, or baby steps, to obey God, but to some a leap and to others a long jump. To some it is a challenge and takes a lot of work, but to others, it just takes a little bit of wrestling with the Holy Spirit. Whatever pace we are in, the truth is that the Bible is full of instructions to obey God for our health and well-being. Since God is the Creator of life, it is beneficial for us to listen to his instructions, for whatever He says is true and it benefits us more than we will ever know. His commandment informs and it teaches us how to live. It is God's instructions for right living, and if we obey there are great rewards.

> The Law of the LORD is perfect, reviving the
> soul;
> The decrees of the LORD are trustworthy, mak-
> ing the wise simple;

> The commandments of the LORD are right,
>   bringing joy to the heart;
> The commandment of the LORD is clear, giving
>   insight to life;
> Reverence to the LORD is pure, lasting forever;
> The laws of the LORD are true; each one is fair.
> They are more desirable than gold, even the fin-
>   est gold.
> They are sweeter also than honey, even honey
>   dripping from the honeycomb.
> They are a warning to those who hear them
> And THERE IS GREAT REWARD FOR
>   THOSE WHO OBEY THEM. (Psalm
>   19:7–11)

Clearly, there are many benefits and advantages in obeying God. One can never lose but instead gain. His laws do not only give insight to life, but it will also make us more intelligent. The intelligence comes from obeying because His laws are full of knowledge, truth, insight, and wisdom. As we have just read, "The decrees of the Lord are trustworthy, making wise the simple." Moreover, in Psalms, it says,

> Your commands make me wiser than my ene-
> mies, for your commands are my constant guide.
> Yes, I have more insight than my teachers. For I
> am always thinking of your decrees. I am even
> wiser than my elders for I have kept your com-
> mandments. I have refused to walk on any path
> of evil, that I may remain obedient to your word.
> (Psalm 119:98–101)

Obedience leads to increase knowledge and understanding for His laws serve as a lamp and a light to the path of right living.

God longs for His children to obey. Parents long for their children to obey. They seek obedience because more often than not, obedience can only lead to good. When our parents tell us to always look both ways before crossing the street, they expect us to obey and more. They expect us to do it every time we cross the street, so we will not get run over. When our parents tell us to stay away from drugs, they mean it with a sincere prayer, a longing hope, and a trembling heart since our health, well-being and success will more than likely depend on it. In the same way, God desires our obedience from His children, for obedience brings blessings and protection. When God says do not cheat, steal, or kill, He is protecting others and us from harm. Obviously, stealing, killing, and the like could put a person in jail, or worse, it could result to death. Obedience to God's commands is a refuge to those who listens. In Psalm 1:3, it says that "but all who listen to me will live in peace and safety, unafraid of harm."

> If you make the LORD your refuge, if you make the Most High your shelter, no evil will conquer you; no plague will come near your dwelling. For He orders His angels to protect you wherever you go... The LORD says, I will rescue those who love me. I will protect those who trust in my name. When they call on me, I will answer; I will be with them in trouble. I will rescue them and honor them. I will satisfy them with a long life and give them my salvation. (Psalm 91)

> The Lord Himself watches over you! The Lord stands beside you as your protective shade. The sun will not hurt you by day, nor the moon at night. The Lord keeps you from evil and preserves your life. The Lord keeps watch over you as you come and go both now and forever. (Psalm 121:5–9)

If it is not obvious yet, obedience to God leads to secure and protected life. It should be clear by now that there are great rewards, blessings, and opportunities when we do what God wants us to do. We grow the most when we acknowledge and abide by the authority that tells us how to live a better life. Moreover, obedience leads to joy, peace of mind, heart, and soul because God specially outpours His grace to His obedient children who empties him or herself to Him.

God longs for you to obey so He can purify your whole heart. Don't allow the bad spirit to hold a grip on you. Do not let the bad spirit blind you of the truth and rob you of God's goodness. You cannot walk with God if you are holding hands with the devil. Take advantage of the great blessings of obedience. Obey and leave whatever is holding you in bondage and be free.

Do not let the bad spirit blind you of the truth and rob you of God's goodness and joy

CHAPTER 6

ABUNDANT LIFE AND FREEDOM

Many do not want to obey or follow Christ's teachings because they seemed to have acquired a knowledge or a belief that a Christian's life has too many restrictions; it has too many do's and don'ts. Some think that if they become a Christian, they would have to give up many things that they usually do. But contrary to this belief, Christian life is actually abundant due to the freedom experienced through obedience.

As you may have already known, God's laws were designed to protect men. The deterrence and restriction comes from protecting others and ourselves from harm. Unlike if men were to make laws, when they do, they end up destroying themselves (for example, legalizing abortion). They already do by not obeying God and by taking matters into their hands. They disobey God's laws and fool around on their spouse, they lie to everyone, and they steal and kill. Taking matters into our hands causes us to injure others and ourselves. God's laws are designed to free humanity; it is not to make our lives burdensome, onerous, or oppressive. Drinking, for instance, is not prohibited to Christians. But early on and until today, some Christians avoid drinking because of the effect of alcohol to an individual. The intoxication effect creates undesirable result such as harm, injury, embarrassments, addiction, and deaths. Drinking gives the impression of a good time, but the eventual consequence is bad times, physical deterioration, and many other woes. Moreover, the impact to friends and families could be devastating, and it could cause broken relationship and financial and legal difficulties.

Self-restrictions are formed and instituted so we can live a life free from addiction, torment, or damage.

Life with God is not full of restrictions; if it is, then nobody would want to become a Christian. But as it is, there are millions, if not billions, of Christians on this planet who enjoy the Christian life. Ritenbaugh explained it well when he said,

> Yet, just because a Christian exercise self-control does not mean his life is boring, underprivileged, and unrewarding. In fact, lived properly, a Christian life is ultimately more exciting, successful, and satisfying than most human beings can imagine! Certainly, the lives of Christians are full of responsibility and self-restraint, but the rewards and blessings that accrue over a lifetime of pleasing God and living His way of life simply overwhelm the seemingly onerous duties and strictures. There is no comparison![6]

"I am going to restrain myself so that I can achieve what is good for me in the long run."

My previous preacher once said, "I am going to restrain myself so that I can achieve what is better for me in the long run." This statement is true and should be taken to heart; if you restrain yourself from sin, you will have a fruitful, successful, and productive life, and you will gain freedom. Allow me to illustrate further. If you restrain from drinking, for instance, you will save money, you will live a healthier life, you will have better relationships, and you will be spared from embarrassments. If you restrain from smoking, you will save money whether through medical bills or through buying cigarettes, you will have more time to spend on productive chores, and you will be spared from addiction. Your life and the lives of others will be spared from cancer or death, and your good friends will come closer to you instead of staying away from you. If you restrain from overeating, you will have a nicer body, you will save money, and you will live longer as well. If you restrain from lying, everyone will trust you, and you will be trusted with valuable things. If you restrain from fooling around on your wife, you will spare your family and yourself from embarrassment, grief, and pain. You avoid going into perhaps bankruptcy, getting STD (sexually transmitted disease), or from the deadening feeling of guilt. You avoid betraying your family, your wife, and your God. Freedom from the bondage of evil things is a wonderful feeling—it is healthy, it makes us wealthy, and it is liberating.

However, I also understand that giving up old, embedded bad habits that have held us in bondage is difficult to overcome. Giving up pornography, for instance, could be difficult since it could take more than time, energy, strength, or will power to do it. God understands; that's why He said, "If anyone wishes to come after Me, let him deny himself and take up his cross daily and follow me. For whoever wishes to save his life shall lose it, but whoever loses his life for My sake, he is the one who will save it (Luke 9:23, 24)." He also said, "The One who is in you is greater than the one who is in the world" (1 John 4:4). Giving up pornography, smoking, or drinking could be a daily struggle, but the reward is freedom and better life. I've also known many who gave up smoking easily. One of my friends in Belgium, in particular, gave up smoking in one day. He was so addicted that he used to smoke two to three packs per day. He said he used to sleep noisily like an old machine, so one day he decided to stop and now he could sleep like a baby.

As you may know by now, the denying of self is not detrimental, but instead, it is advancing oneself. Believe me when I say God's way is the right way. The real meaning of life is found by losing yourself to God. This is a personal choice that easily leads to victory. You can only gain; you cannot lose anything. If you deny yourself and keep from doing the things that could harm your body and soul and the people close to you, then you will have a rewarding victory. If you give up the things that keeps God away, and if you take away the things that keeps you from following God, then you will find the true meaning of freedom.

The thou shall nots are clear instructions and guidance that frees us from sin and the deadening conscience of guilt. Not obeying these instructions is rebelling and rejecting God, rather than being led by God.

Yes, it is true that a Christian life has many restrictions, but these restrictions are for the sake of our well-being. The commandment is a lamp and the light, and the reproofs for discipline are the way of life (Proverbs 6:23). It comes from the love of self and others. It is not designed to make our life complex or onerous; instead, it is designed to keep us from evil and harm. It is designed to guard us from harmful desires. It is the road that deprives oneself of wrong but gain the true way of living. It is designed to achieve better lives, to gain self-control, right conduct, and a devotion to God. It is designed to achieve freedom from bondage and addiction and to allow us to experience the meaning of being truly free.

CHAPTER 7

ABUNDANT LIFE THROUGH CHALLENGING TIMES

Life on this planet is not immune to struggles, stress, despair, uncertainties, or anxieties that challenge our emotional well-being. In order to make life abundant during these times, we need to accept and understand that these challenging times are part of life. These challenging situations happen to teach us about life and about ourselves. They teach us how to deal with difficult situations. They teach us how to deal with emotions, how to cope with stress, how to meet challenges, or how to solve problems. These setbacks are opportunities to manage our emotions, to become resilient, to learn and grow in the process. They can help us grow in wisdom, knowledge, understanding, or to become mature. The opportunity to experience pain is an opportunity. It is an opportunity to rise above, to set ourselves up on higher ground.

The decisions and choices that we make in everyday circumstances, for instance, could make us better or worse. Life is often reflected on the decisions and the choices that we make. Everyone knows that decisions that we make have positive and negative consequences. The difficult decision we face every day to be free from the bondage of sin, alcohol, drugs, or any addictive substance, for instance, is a decision that contributes to a better life. Deciding not to be free is always damaging, unhealthy, and harmful. Even simple decisions such as choosing which movie to watch can be difficult and complex. But making decisions during challenging times may even be more difficult since we are vulnerable to irrational or illogical thinking and judgments. However, we often have time to decide what to do when faced with these circumstances. We have time to decide if we want to buy another dose or not. We have time to think if we should steal or not. And during these deciding moments, reflecting on the consequence of our past, present, and future actions could always help in making better judgements. The choice to make our life and other lives better is always the better choice. It is always better to handle life's problems with wisdom with positive outcomes than solve it with negative consequences.

Life is not easy due to the many challenges we encounter every day. I like to refer to them occasionally as "bumps" because these situations do challenge our beings. It challenges who we are, what we are made of, and what our entire reason for existence is. It affects our decision processes, and sometimes, it bumps, or jolts, us out of our comfort zones. Some of these times are bearable, but some, if not most, are unpleasant and unwanted; some are self-inflicted, some are accidents, and some are natural occurrences. But it is a fact that these challenging times are a part of life, and our response to them could make us stand or stumble. It is a reality that people get sick, people die, accidents happen, jobs are dispensable, and people do or say things that hurt other people.

Let us further lay other foundation and illustrate some of the causes of miseries that will help us understand and put challenging times into perspective. Adverse circumstances happen because of the following reasons:

- *We do it to ourselves.* Miseries happen because we sometimes make wrong decisions or do things that cause pain; we sin, we make wrong choices, and we say or do things that hurt ourselves and others.
- *Others did it.* The choices and decisions of other people causes pain. They, for instance, drink and drive, they bomb buildings, and they batter their spouse, causing adversity, misery, and lives. They also say or do things that pierce

their love ones' hearts. We also live in a fallen world with the devil. Satan constantly attacks humanity, causing us to hurt each other.

- *It is an accident.* Sometimes things happen beyond our control. A warning sign, for instance, fell or was blown away, causing undesirable accident.

- *Ignorance, or we do not know.* Unknowingly, we sometimes eat contaminated food without knowing that it will make us sick. Sometimes we say or do things that hurt others without even knowing its impact.

- *It is a natural phenomenon.* A person goes in for a regular doctor's checkup only to find out that he or she has cancer. A flood or tornado could destroy houses or cars.

These causes illustrate that sometimes things happen under our control and sometimes it is beyond our control. Regardless, most of the above causes are unpleasant and unwanted since they can hurt, and they can affect our psychological and physiological well-being. Hence, consciously and diligently watching ourselves to avoid, and manage what we can control can help escape pain, sorrow, regret, or the deadening power of guilt.

Most of the challenges in life are under our control. They are manageable especially if we allow the Holy Spirit to take control of our life. Our decision to stop addiction, for instance, is under our control. It is a difficult process, but it is doable and manageable. Many get over it with the help of the Holy Spirit or if they put their mind to it. Fooling around could be avoided if we decide at the beginning not to hurt our spouse or if we decide to stop right away since it is wrong and the ramifications could be grave. The decision not to drink and drive is under our control. The decision not to run the red light is under our control. The decision not to break the law is under control. When we let ourselves out of control, then negative consequences could happen. My friend was hospitalized because a speeding car hit her. The firefighters and police had to break her out of the car, and a helicopter had to fly her to the hospital. The accident devastated her, causing major injuries. What happened was out of her control, but the person who hit her could have prevented the accident by not speeding.

But some of the pain and suffering are unavoidable and beyond our control. As illustrated above, some of the pain and suffering are accidental or due to ignorance or natural phenomenon. But these instances could be managed if we understand that there may be a reason or a cause for the phenomenon. These undesirable circumstances may be necessary to teach us about something that we are not aware about.

There is beauty that comes out from thorns and thistles

Pain and Suffering Are Sometimes Necessary

Some of life's complications are sometimes necessary for abundant life. These challenging times are essential since oftentimes they can mold our character if we do not allow it to break us. These bumps can build our character if we don't let it ruin our lives. Punishing a child for stealing, for instance, could save him from imprisonment or from committing crime in the future. To get the impurities out of the gold, it has to be heated, and to form and mold a metal, it has to be heated on fire. In the same way, these challenging times could refine our character if we learn from it and allow it to mold us. If we allow it to change us, then "we can rejoice, too, when we run into problems and trials, for we know that they are good for us—they help us learn to endure. And endurance develop strength of character in us" (Romans 5:3–5).

Endurance is one of the characters that we can develop, bring about, or strengthen further during these hard times. It is a positive and admirable character that gives the capacity to undergo adverse circumstances with hope and determination despite disappointments, rejections, and persecutions. Endurance acknowledges the situation and continues with life even under resistance. It requires that we withstand pressure, pain, annoyance, hardships, or challenges with calmness and patience. Enduring the resistance of addiction, refusing to give in or take another dose or shot, for instance, will help us build a stronger character. When we learn to be strong and steadfast in these circumstances, we mature, we grow, we learn, we get wisdom, and we become successful, just like when we enter into a competition in the Olympics or when we go to school. Enduring the grueling pain of training could fashion us to become strong and successful. Enduring many years of education—studying for tests, defying temptations, ignoring bullies, putting up with teachers that do not know how to teach—helps us to mature, to grow in wisdom and knowledge, to be successful, to be understanding, and to become a better person. Also, knowing that God will and is always going to be there no matter the challenges we face should give us peace.

Understanding Pain and Suffering through Faith

God is still in control regardless of what we are going through. So this is the time to rely on Him more. He sees every aspect of our situations and disappointments. But He still loves us regardless of our failures and frustrations. We may not understand why things happen, but oftentimes they are for our good or for the advancement of His kingdom. John Bunyan is one of the few who understand the positive outcome of challenging situations. As a result, he welcomes the situation. He said,

> God sends things that take from us everything for which our physical natures long, things like sickness, losses, crosses, persecution, and troubles—and usually these, though they shock us whenever they happen, carry blessings to help us. For God make us fruitful in the land of affliction... I have often realized, sorrow is better than laughter, for sadness has a refining influence on us.

Life anchored in Christ can weather the storm

John Bunyan goes further to say, "I wouldn't be surprised if there were some people who would say that their days of trouble were their best days." Reminiscing Psalms, "The people who go down into the deeps, living their lives in the midst of the flood, they are the ones who most clearly see the wonderful works of the Lord" (Psalm 107:23–24).

Paul understood this profound situation as well. He pleaded God three times to remove his pain. But God refused, and Paul said,

> And He said to me "My grace is sufficient for you, for My strength is made perfect in weakness." Therefore, most gladly I will rather boast in my infirmities, that the power of Christ may rest upon me. Therefore, I take pleasure in infirmities, in reproaches, in needs, in persecutions, in distresses, for Christ's sake. For when I am weak then I am strong.

God usually works when we are weak because in these situations we cannot rely on our own strengths but on God's. And it is almost always true that the only time we realize that we need God is when something dramatic happens in our life. Unfortunately, the great need is the only encouragement that drives us to God. The desperate plea for healing and solution is focused on God because we know that He is the only one who can fix our situation. This is where faith comes in. When the earth shakes around us and everything falls apart, we simply trust when there's nothing but God to hold on to.

However, one should not easily attribute suffering as God's doing since as outlined early on, there are many causes of suffering. God is not in the business of ruining lives; He is in the business of building lives. But if suffering is the only way to build our character, then He may allow it to happen. But one may ask, why would a good God allow evil or suffering? There are many theological and philosophical answers written for this difficult question. However, as you already know, my answer would be "to save our life" or "to help us grow." In addition, it can also be out of our control, it is a phenomenon, or He has a better plan than we do." It seems cruel for God to allow pain and suffering just to teach us a lesson, but sometimes it is the only way. He is more interested in helping us go through with it so we can grow and learn. God may have something greater in store for us, and sometimes it may not be for us but for the advancement of His kingdom. We may not fully understand, but challenging times do bring about something good in God's kingdom and in our life, like the ultimate good that parents desire in punishing a child. It seems cruel, but sometimes the only way we see light is when we have seen darkness. The only way we know what is good is when we know what is bad. As some have said, he who suffers most has the most to give. Understand that God allows pain to cause you to stand. The devil, on the other hand, sends pain to cause you to stumble.

Again, pain and suffering are not God's ultimate desire but our well-being. As you already know, He healed the sick, the lame, and the blind and raised the dead back to life. He created commandments to keep us from pain and suffering. The "thou shall nots" are life's instructions to make living peaceful.

However, some may cringe and may not understand and see the hand of God during these times. But one should trust the Lord always because God always wants the best for His children regardless of the situation they are in. That's why the godly give thanks to the Almighty for the challenging times because they see the light that shines upon them. Sometimes they do not understand, but they do know that God is with them. They would see His footsteps in the sand, and in the midst of challenging times, they would always remember that joy, pleasure, success, laughter, contentment, and happiness would come. They understand that good and bad comes hand in hand in this life and it is through challenging times that they are able to grow and see the hand of God in their lives. They understand that a life anchored in Christ can weather the storm and they will come out with it better than before the storm. Cry or call on God for help, healing, or solution, and observe what He has planned for you.

Preparing Self for Afflictions

In addition to trusting the Lord, it is also important to educate and prepare oneself for most of these circumstances before, during, or after it happens. Preparing oneself makes challenging times bearable, confrontable, and oftentimes avoidable. If we educate ourselves with communicable diseases, for instance, and if we avoid active sexual lifestyle that could inflict sexually transmitted diseases, then we shun damage or devastation. If we educate ourselves with the damaging effects of drugs, alcohol, or any addictive substance, then we could potentially avoid temptation and the devastating effects of addiction. If we avoid from overeating, especially sweets and fatty foods, then we will stay healthy and avoid sickness such as diabetes or heart disease. The loss of job is another example; the loss does not have to be so painful if we have saved some money to live on for months. Some financial advisors suggest saving six to twelve months of living expenses, other experts suggest three or more. More importantly, by educating ourselves, we are able to transcend or come out with it normally than we could have been.

It is important to learn and avoid these circumstances, but learning God's intent for our life is even more critical. Educating ourselves with spiritual wisdoms can prepare us to stand when a hurricane of life comes. Asking for God's help usually makes challenging times bearable. It helps us keep our emotions in check when anger or temptation are dominating our day. God's words are weapons of our warfare. Memorizing, reading, and relying on God's word is one of the most critical weapons when we are in this valley of life. David, in Psalm 23:4, said, "Even though I walk through the valley of the shadow of death, I will fear no evil, for you are with me; your rod and your staff, they comfort me." In Psalm 119:18, 24, he also said, "Open my eyes, that I may behold wonderful things from your law… Your testimonies also are my delight; they are my counselors."

It is important to prepare and learn to avoid or manage these circumstances, but understanding why it is happening is equally important.

The Relevance of Understanding Pain

It is also important to know, realize, understand, and accept these situations in order to manage or ease the pain. Knowing that you are not in this situation indefinitely—realizing that this is a part of life and, just like everything else, this too shall pass—could help us understand and rationalize the situation. Problems do not usually come to stay; they come and go. Also, recognizing that what happened could or could not have been avoided helps us make sense of these situations. It makes us understand that what happened has already happened, and it may be that nothing we do will change the situation.

But some are in these unpleasant situations for a long time or indefinitely because they fail to realize that this is a normal part of living, and they certainly would not accept the situation. Nevertheless, if we are aware when we are in this dilemma, then we should realize, understand, and decide to accept these challenges and choose to solve it or move on. And when we do, the pain becomes manageable, we become stronger, and as mentioned above, this could be an opportunity to build character. Again, these challenging times are a part of life, and they will not go away. So either we manage it and move on or be depressed about it. As some say, make lemonades out of lemons. Others say, either keep busy dying or keep busy living.

Grieving, for instance, is one of the most difficult problems that we encounter in our lifetime. Almost all of us, if not all, will encounter grieving, and when we do, taking a little time to reflect on the situation could help. Perhaps the first step could be to accept that this is a normal life situation—meaning it happens to everyone, and it will happen whether now or in the future. We may not be ready for it to happen, but it will or it just happens. The next step could be to understand that we are grieving, and hence, we might need to talk to a counselor or search the Internet about grieving processes. There are steps to grieving and psychological and physiological awareness that we might need to know in order to understand the pain of losing someone we love. Understanding and educating ourselves helps us to recognize that our pain is normal. The valuable information that we obtain can help us make sense of our emotions and experiences. And in the future, because of the knowledge and experiences, the next grieving would perhaps not be so bad. What's more, we are able to help and empathize with others who might need our support in the future.

Defying Pain

Pain is easier for most Christians because we have Christ in us to help us through the situation. I believe that God instilled a stronger character within us, such as endurance and the courage to move on, that could win above the negative feeling that pulls us down. I believe that God created us to triumph and not fail. We should not allow the pain to be the center of our being, but the positive internal thinking that we have within should be the core of our being. As the saying goes, we should not allow defeat to defeat us. God usually help His children go through challenging times, and sometimes God heals physically, internally, and spiritually.

Pain Could Be an Opportunity

These unpleasant situations should also be an opportunity to get closer to God. Instead of blaming God or asking God why it is happening, we should take this as an opportunity because it is our chance to rely on the Lord for love, comfort, healing, and grace. I will keep repeating myself when I say that abundant life is only possible when we live our lives through Christ because these challenging times become bearable through Him. The safest place to be when we are in this situation is in the arms of Christ. God's children are blessed with God's grace in time of need, in time of trials, tribulations, hardships, grieving, failures and so on. Whenever God's children get hit with one of these undesirable bumps they run to Christ for healing, direction, wisdom, comfort, and grace. He is the only one they trust to give guidance and comfort or ease the pain in these dire situations.

To illustrate, our accountant's wife passed away in early 2000. He was grieving immensely for his wife. His wife was his life and joy. To him his life and joy was gone, and the pain was tremendous. I remember exactly what he told to my husband and me when we went there a month or so after his wife's death. With tears in his eyes, he said, "Grieving is painful, and fortunately for us Christians, we have God and His grace to help us go through this process. But I do not know or even imagine how non-Christians go through it without the grace of God." Life can be difficult, but it is even more difficult without God, who gives inner peace and comfort. He usually doesn't remove suffering, but He soothes away the pain that no one can ever do. True Christians experience the grace that is from God alone, and this goes beyond human understanding. Jesus said, "I am leaving you with a gift—peace of mind and heart. And the peace I give isn't like the peace the world gives" (John 14:27).

Another illustration was when I was going through my college years. At that time, I was attending university part time (oftentimes full time), working twenty to forty hours a week, and taking care of my family's needs all at the same time. With this heavy and busy schedule, I even had time to go to church every Sunday, read the Bible, and pray almost every day. I had two teenagers who were in high school and college and a husband who was battling depression and attending seminary at the same time. As a typical mom, I did all the house chores, including cleaning, cooking, buying grocery, doing the laundry, etc. I did not realize how difficult my life had been, not until someone asked me, "How did *you* do it? How did *you* manage to take care of your family's needs, work, go to school, and even manage to get As and Bs in your grades?" (I only had one C' on my transcript.) The only response that I could think of was, "I did it through God's grace."

My accountant had gone through grieving with peace because of focusing on God and relying on His grace and comfort. He grieved with peace and comfort because he knew that his wife is in better hands; she is in heaven with Christ. He knew the meaning of "to live is Christ." He focused on God instead of his circumstances. I had gone through college years with peace in my heart because of the same focus, grace, and love. Because God is our God, we were able to rely on Him to overcome these difficult situations with lightness, serenity, and comfort. I once heard a speaker who said, "A life on the edge with God is better than being in the comfort zone without God." With God, living through challenging situations is much easier than going through it without Him. This is because God intends to mold us and not hurt us; He intends for us to have abundant life.

Another Unique Opportunity

One of the opportunities that we have when in this situation is to weather the storm with calm and grace. We could even have fun while in the middle of the pain. I was listening to a preacher in Dallas, Texas, who was preaching about suffering one day. He said, "Suffering is not the absence of goodness, but where the true beauty lies."

I grew up in a place where flood is a seasonal problem. I used to live in a two-story house, and every year our house would get flooded due to the storm. The flood would reach the first floor, and we would then move to the second floor. Sometimes, the second floor gets flooded as well, and we would then have to move out of the house and go to an evacuation area, usually a school or a gym close by. Our parents would grieve and feel sad since most of our furnishings would get damaged or lost. They detested the moving of all of our belongings from place to place. Some would prepare for the storm and leave ahead of time, and some, like my parents, would wait until the last minute, hoping and praying that we would not have to leave. But to us children, we rejoice because we do not have to go to school. It was an opportunity for us to run around and play under the rain. We used to love it!

Sometimes we are in this situation for the benefit of ourselves. When we are sick, for instance, it may be an opportunity to rest and catch up on good books that we have been putting off reading. Sometimes our body just needs healing through rest.

The Preciousness of Life

My husband once asked me one of the most difficult questions that I thought I would never have to answer. He said, "What would you do to someone who is in constant pain and who want nothing else but end the pain by dying? Will you allow this person to die just to end the pain and suffering?" My answer was *no*. I would never allow someone to die just to end his or her suffering. If a person is in constant pain, there are many medications that are available to relieve the pain, and a request for death is out of the question.

However, there are some who would perhaps make the difficult decision of ending someone's life. Unfortunately, sometimes, some of us are faced with undesirable situations where taking our life or someone's life is easier and a more convenient choice than saving life. Most of the time, this choice is due to financial burden that the sick person imposes. Unfortunately, we and our system have imposed monetary value on life. Some of us are aware about Terri Schiavo's case. I was in Canada when I heard a debate about her situation. The debate was about a person who was in the hospital for a period of time and the tubes were the only things keeping her alive. Some of the taxpayers were complaining that their tax dollars should not be wasted if the person would die soon anyway. However, that "soon" could take months or perhaps one or more years. But money should not be the motive for taking one's life; it should not even be a debate. Hospitals and doctors are there to save lives and not take them away, and that's the way it should be. Cost should not be the basis of life. A system's decision should not be the basis of taking someone's life. But the value of life in itself should be the basis of saving life.

People have timelines. We are all terminal; we all die. We do not know when, but we will die. We could die tomorrow, next month, or next year. So should we take a life because we are terminal? However difficult or inconvenient a sick person brings, it is still a life, a precious life that we are deciding to end. One should understand that there is always a glimmer of hope for a better life that the person in despondence is not aware about. The person in pain is not able to rationally think for himself and is unable to envision the future of a pain free life since he or she is only focused on the current condition. But even for a person relying on tubes alone, his or her life is precious and should be valued.

My mother told me once an awesome story about her neighbor. Her neighbor's wife was diagnosed with cancer and eventually passed away. But before the wife went to heaven, the husband stayed in the hospital for several months trying to save her life. My mother was very impressed at how the husband took care of his wife during those difficult times. Every day for several months, he would go to the hospital after work to check on his wife and then later would go home to attend to his children's needs and then go back to the hospital to sleep in his wife's bedside and then wake up and go to work the next morning. After the wife passed away, my mother asked him how did he do it. My mother asked, "How is it that you were able to do all this?" He said, "I was able to do all those things because I have set in my mind that my wife is Jesus. I set my mind on taking care of not my wife but Jesus." Now if the Son of God, Jesus, is the life that you are deciding to end, would you pull the plug? This is a difficult question. But here's the answer—Jesus said, "I tell you the truth, whatever you did for one of the least of these brothers of mine, you did for me" (Matthew 25:40).

But allow me for a moment to respond to the question that my husband asked about pain and suffering. My father had gone through this kind of pain. He experienced pain that no one in this world should ever have to experience. He used to work on an oil tanker with an oil company in the Philippines. One day, while docked on the pier for repairs, the oil tanker that he was working on exploded. My father was the only survivor because he was thrown to the water during the explosion. All his co-workers died before reaching the hospital. He was thrown off the tanker but not without 95 percent of his body getting burned. All the skin around his face, neck, head, and body was burned; he suffered third-degree burns. The only part of his body that had skin that was intact was on his legs. The doctors even had to graft the skin that was left on his legs to patch his severely burnt stomach.

At the hospital, only a few of my father's immediate family were allowed to visit since he was highly susceptible to infection. Only a few of us saw his naked body inside an incubator that kept his body warm. Only a few of us witnessed his tremendous pain, his delirious and seemingly dying state. He lay naked since he could not bear the pain of anything near his body. The pain was so severe he went into a state of delirium for several weeks. Everyone who had seen him thought that he would not survive. I myself thought the same thing, although I had a glimmer of hope since I prayed to God. Also, my dad has been known to be like a cat—he has nine lives. He had gone through many accidents, including being shot during the war (he was almost a teenager then) and his arms getting caught in between vehicles, almost losing his right arm, but he always somehow manage to pull through. Nevertheless, at the hospital, the doctors concluded that if his delirious state would continue in a week or two, then his insanity would be permanent. To burn a small portion of one's body seems unbearable, but imagine your whole body. Imagine the endless pain.

My father survived, but his fingers became stiff, shriveled, and disfigured. Miraculously, his sanity was back after three weeks, and he was able to live an almost normal life again. My father survived because doctors, nurses, and his family loved, cared, and prayed. He survived because everyone around him were patient and ignored his occasional plea of death and difficult personality (that was due to his pain), and that made his recovery even more difficult. But once recovered, regardless of his deformities, he was back to his old self— always happy, always smiling, always looking for ways to brighten his and someone else's day.

My father had gone through tremendous pain that seemed endless. He survived because there was a glimmer of hope, even though everyone thought that there was none. Our inconveniences are nothing compared to the preciousness of life. Suffering does not diminish the dignity of a person. That's why euthanasia is never, in my opinion, an option since the value of life is priceless, more costly than gold or money. It is a precious gift from God for us to nurture. Life is not abundant if we do not value the value of life.

Life is invaluable that many people, such as soldiers, are willing to die to preserve other people lives. Some spouse would give their life for their partners. Parents would sacrifice their lives for their children, and some children would do anything to save their parents. When I found out about my father's accident, I prayed to God for his life. I begged God to allow him to live in exchange for my lifetime service and devotion. I almost went to a convent to fulfill this promise. But God had other plans for me. However, the point I am trying to make here is that most people will sacrifice or give up their life to save another life. This is how precious one's life is, and a decision to end one's life should not be taken lightly.

Our life is so valuable that Jesus, the Son of God, died for our sake. He said, "I am the good shepherd. The good shepherd lays down his life for the sheep" (John 10:11). I will keep repeating myself when I say that a life is priceless. My husband was explaining once, in philosophical terms, the value of human life. I did not understand his deep and profound thought and language. Whenever I get into this situation, I usually ask him to explain it to me as if I am in the first grade. So he picked up one of our children's picture when they were adorable little kids and asked me, "If I were to buy this picture from you, what is the cost? What is the price of this picture?" I thought, if I have to lose a valuable irreplaceable picture, then it might as well be expensive. So I said, "One thousand dollars." Then his next question was, "Now if I want to buy your children from you and do to them whatever I want to do, what is the cost? How much are your children worth to you?" I was speechless; I could not come out with an amount or numerical value. In my mind, I was thinking five million, ten million, fifteen million. But I finally gave up and realized that they are priceless, they are invaluable, and this is what my husband was trying to explain. So I finally said, "There is no amount of money that can buy them." He said, "You got it." Humans are *very* special no one should ever think of taking one's precious life. Sometimes we tend to forget that our life is costly that the Son of God gave His life for our lives.

Allow me for a moment to illustrate further the value of life. One of my closest relatives asked me in the past if she should have an abortion since she and her husband were in the process of having a divorce and she was three months pregnant. Her husband committed adultery, and he admitted to not changing his lifestyle, so she decided to end the relationship. During the divorce process, her husband was trying to convince her to have an abortion since he claimed that no man would want to marry her if she had a child. I convinced her to keep the baby. I was thinking of what my mother told me and my sister when we were teenagers. She told us to never ever have an abortion if we get pregnant. To make the story short, she went ahead with the pregnancy and had a handsome adorable boy. Her son became her joy without any remorse, and she dated several men before eventually getting married again. After about seven years, the father of the boy decided to finally visit his son. I then told her to introduce the boy and tell him "Here he is. Now kill him!" I may have been out of place in saying this, but the reality is life is precious, born or unborn. A baby is a person—it is innocent and is valuable whether it is inside or outside the womb. A decision to end the life of an unborn child is not humane. My husband told me once that "there is one thing worse than slavery and that is killing an innocent."

Oftentimes, we take lightly the value of life, not realizing its immense worth. Here are some questions to help us understand further the cost of human life. Would you trade your hands for a million dollars? You would not be able to do many things like give yourself a bath or clean yourself after using the toilet, but would you trade your two hands for the right price? Would you trade a million dollars for your feet that are valuable for walking, running, climbing, or dancing with your loved one? Some of you probably said, "No way." But some of you would probably trade your body parts for good reasons. But if you imagine your life without hands or legs, you will probably say "no way" as well. I myself will not trade any of them, not even for two million dollars. I would rather have hands to eat, drive, and give myself a bath than have millions. I would rather have feet that give me the freedom and the pleasure to roam around than have money but be in misery. The point I am trying to make is that, if our body parts are costly, how much worth is it for a life.

Understand that the preciousness of life is what makes life abundant. Just look at an innocent baby. Life itself is precious, it is valuable, it is a privilege, it is a gift.

Imagine for a moment that you are something other than human. Imagine, for instance, that you are a dog watching and observing the lives of humans who own you. Your owners are materialistic, harsh, selfish, self-conceited and are always fighting. One particular day, the parents were fighting and yelling, and the children were crying and sad. A few minutes later, the husband decides to leave with his belongings. This time, the children are not only crying but are now hurting and getting confused as well. As a dog, you will probably nod your head in frustration and say, "They should try to be me for a month. Maybe they will realize the value of being human. Maybe they will realize the privilege, the joy, the opportunities, and the difference that they can make to make this world a better place to be. Maybe they will learn how to love and care and realize that what they are fighting about is nothing compared to being a dog. Maybe they will realize that the life that they have is good and awesome. If only I could trade places with the father. Maybe he will wake up and realize what a fool this has all been. Maybe he will realize that human life is worth celebrating. And having a family is even better. Oh, the privilege of raising the children! Oh the joy of playing with them! Oh, the challenge to make them better people! Oh the privilege." Many of us miss out on these privileges because we devalue the gift of life. If you are one of those who do not realize the worth of human life, try being a dog, a fish, or a tree for a month sometime.

Abundant life on earth does not mean prosperity and happiness all the time. It also includes inconsistencies and challenges that are often reflected from the decisions and choices that we make. But this life's bumps do not have to be so painful if we decide to educate, understand, and prepare ourselves for these situations. It is manageable if we understand that this is a part of life that needs solution or a part of life that produces opportunities. Moreover, these challenging times could be handled better and easier if we value the preciousness of life.

These challenging times could be handled better if we value the preciousness of life

My relative's decision to keep her child, for instance, allowed her the opportunity to experience the joy and challenges of having a child. It also allowed her to leave the negative behind and opened herself up to another life's adventures. Her decision made her a better person because she was able to rise above her emotion and the challenges that could have pulled her down. The most important point I want to impart is "Do not quit." Try and weather the storm with calm and grace. Just like what Jesus did when He was in a boat with His disciples in the middle of the storm—Jesus was asleep while His disciples were frantic.

For Christians, what makes life abundant in the midst of these challenges is the grace and love that God has provided for His children. In Matthew 11:28–30, God said, "Come to me, all who labor and are heavy laden, and I will give you rest. Take My yoke upon you and learn from Me, for I am gentle and lowly in heart, and you will find rest for your souls. For My yoke is easy and My burden is light."

CHAPTER 8

HEALTH IS WEALTH

I shall also add that a good health could help us avoid some of the pain and suffering that we encounter in life. Sickness can negatively affect the spiritual, emotional, and mental areas of our life. It could take away our abundant life. Hence, recognizing the importance of good health in the midst of everyday living is important. Keeping our body healthy helps us to appreciate the wealth we have that we often ignore. Our good health is a valuable capital that needs to be nurtured. If we do not realize the wealth of being healthy or if we take for granted and undervalue our health, then we miss out on the real value of good health to life. We would fail to realize that our good health is a big contributor to abundant living. It is so valuable that if we were inflicted with disease like AIDS or heart disease, our life would feel like it is going down the drain. It would shock, overwhelm, or devastate us. It would feel like our good life is about to end, and we then start to feel miserable. We would perhaps feel anger, disbelief, worry, or fear.

Health is invaluable that even a Hindu boy understands. Below is a poem he wrote while in school.

> Health is wealth
> Money isn't real wealth.
> Don't collect only wealth,
> It might spoil your health.

Don't spoil your health
By thinking about wealth.
Always have good health
Which is the real wealth.[7]

A healthy body is indeed a wealth that we oftentimes undermine. If we stop for a moment and think and take an inventory of the wealth that our healthy body contributes to abundant life, we might be amazed at how wealthy we are, and we might become more conscious at keeping it in shape. Compared to the blind, for instance, a person with good eyesight is fortunate and far more blessed. A person with healthy legs and feet is more favorable than the one in a wheelchair. But however weird as it may seem, even a person inflicted with AIDS, at some point, thanked this disease that came into his life. He said that without aids he could not have realized the preciousness of life.

One must know the value of good health because abundant life is augmented with good health. The old saying above that "Health is wealth" is true and should not be undermined. Allow me to keep repeating that diseases such as cancer, AIDS, or cardiovascular problems can sap our strength, our joy, or our well-being. It could cause misery, suffering, anguish, or grief. Taking into consideration the high cost of health care nowadays, a sickness could cost us everything we have and more. Hence, one should value good health, and it should be nourished and taken care of to enjoy a healthy lifestyle.

Nowadays there are many things to keep in mind in order to keep our body healthy. There are many vitamins that are recommended for good health, and there are many diets that claim to be the one. One of my longtime friends in Belgium once suggested what I thought to be a sound strategy to diet. She said, "Someone once said, 'Eat like a king for breakfast, like a queen at lunch, and like a pauper at dinner.'" I thought this was a good suggestion. I actually tried it, but I ended up doing the opposite. I kept going back to my usual diet. I ate like a queen in the morning, like a queen in the afternoon, and like a king at night. However, many doctors, counselors, and health experts would perhaps agree on three things, and that is to exercise regularly, have plenty of fresh fruits and vegetables, and eat or drink in moderation.

Good nutrition is invaluable to a healthy lifestyle. God created many delicious fruits and vegetables because in the beginning, the Creator meant for us to eat fresh and stay healthy (Daniel 1:11–16). Eating healthy, in my opinion, means eating fresh foods, although I myself admit that I do sometimes eat preserved food. I also realize that there is no comparison to eating a home-cooked meal. From my own experience, the more I eat healthy foods, the healthier I feel, and the more junk food I put into my body, the crappier (excuse the language, please) I feel. I was watching a television show about dieting, and the guest was someone who lost about a hundred pounds. She said something that I thought was interesting, "I lost weight because every time I put something in my mouth, I asked myself a question, 'Is this good for my body?'" Ironically, some of us do have to ask ourselves the same question since what we deposit into our bodies do affect our life. I believe that our body was designed to process fresh food. When we continually put something processed such as food preservatives, additives, or chemicals that our system does not recognize, then our precious bodies eventually malfunction, and diseases such as cancer, obesity, diabetes, or heart problems, develop.

In addition to eating healthy, moderation is, in my opinion, the other important key to a healthy diet. Nowadays, we eat or drink in excess of what the body needs. We take in large amount of our favorites, whether it is wine, chocolate, steak, or soda. While eating breakfast one day, my husband asked me an interesting question. He said, "I wonder if God will judge us one day for eating more than what we should be eating. It seems like it should be along the line of alcoholism or smoking." This may be true since we are commanded to glorify God in our bodies and in spirit (1 Corinthians 6:20). But the fact is that some people are overweight because of harmful eating habits. I say harmful because we are ruining our bodies when we overeat or overdrink. Solomon, the wisest man that ever lived, strongly suggested drastic measures against gluttony. He said, "Stick a knife in your throat if you have a big appetite." I have to confess that I myself enjoy eating good food. But are we doing right to the temple of the Holy Spirit? Food was created for us to nourish our bodies and to enjoy as well, but we should also exercise self-control for a better body, better health, and better life. The saying "To eat to live" makes more sense than "To live to eat." However, it is also understood that some are overweight because of physiological problems, but most are overweight because we overeat, and we have wealth within our means to spend on food.

Health experts also recommend that we add exercise to eating healthy and in moderation to our daily routine. Nowadays, good health is impossible to maintain without exercise, especially for those who have jobs that require them to sit all day long. I believe that we were created to constantly move, just like in the beginning; people walked and exerted energy by tilling the land or hunting for food. Nowadays since we have cars to take us to places, and we have prepared food, exercise becomes a necessity. It is vital and essential since exercise tones or keeps our muscles healthy. Exercise boosts our energy levels, helps fight diseases, promotes better sleep, helps keep our brain healthy, and helps us maintain a healthy weight. A good health is truly a wealth.

CHAPTER 9

LIFE AND WEALTH

Some of my friends and relatives argue that having a lot of money could make life abundant. They claim that if they could buy anything they want, then life is good. This is perhaps true to some; however, I would also argue to the contrary. Most of the rich are abundant with monies, properties, perhaps fame and power, but they also live in loneliness and misery. They have money and physical wealth beyond their need, but they feel empty and unhappy.

Wealth, oftentimes alienates friends and relatives, especially to someone who got lucky and became wealthy instantly. The wealthy sometimes think that their relatives come to them only when they need something like money. Moreover, their wealth escalates them to new social strata, and hence, the poor is no longer within their clique or circle. The affluent then distance themselves from the disadvantaged, losing friends and relatives who were once fun to be with. The poor relatives, on the other hand, think that they are no longer recognized by their wealthy relative. Hence, both camps alienate each other, and the good and happy relationship they previously had is gone.

Some of the wealthy people I know have miserable lives. Celebrities for instance, have money and fame, but they are also famous for having broken families. Their marriages constantly fail, and they are sometimes hooked to drugs and alcohol. Serge Gainsbourg, for instance, a successful French poet, singer-songwriter, actor, and director in France wistfully said some time ago, "J'ai tout reussi sauf ma vie," meaning, "I have made a success of everything except my life." He was wealthy and famous, but in the end, he realized that he had left a legacy that was controversial. He would show up unshaven, drunk, and make controversial remarks on talk shows. Although successful, he failed to experience success in finding a full and meaningful life.

The Scripture illustrates it well, "Those who want to be rich fall into temptation, a trap, and many foolish and harmful desires, which plunge them into ruin and destruction. For the love of money is a root of all kinds of evil, and by craving it, some have wandered away from the faith and pierced themselves with many pains (1 Timothy 6:9–10)." I see this over and over again. Because of the love of money (and notice the verse says, "the love of money" and not just money in itself), some people will kill, cheat, and steal. They may succeed, but while they do, they make a failure of their own lives. Some, if not most, businessmen are notorious for this. They are perceived as successful, but we learn later that they cheated to achieve their goal. And some of them, especially in their old age, will realize that their successes haven't really given them the true and significant meaning of life. The love of money cannot give abundant life. That is why scripture says, "Do not wear yourself out to get rich; have the wisdom to show restraint. Cast but a glance at riches, and they are gone, for they will surely sprout wings and fly off to the sky like an eagle" (Proverbs 23:4–5). Do not be deceived. "True humility and fear of the LORD lead to riches, honor, and long life" (Proverbs 22:1).

Solomon, the richest man alive in his time, had seven hundred wives and three hundred concubines, and yet he considered everything vanity. To King Solomon, our relationship with God is the only thing that matters. He said, "Fear God and keep His commandments, for this is man's all" (Ecclesiastes 12:13). He considers this the most important thing because he knew that wealth can never make a man wealthy and that what really makes a man wealthy is having a meaningful relationship with God and man, as we shall see later.

However, I also understand that wealth can contribute to abundant life. But I will keep repeating myself when I say that wealth alone cannot make our life abundant. Having material wealth can never satisfy us. We always want a bigger and better television. We always want a bigger and better house. We always want a more expensive car, jewelry, clothes, and the list goes on. These acquisitions will only make us happy for a short period of time. The happiness here is fleeting and not meaningful.

God is not opposed to having wealth. Many biblical characters were wealthy, like Solomon, Abraham, and Job, but their relationship with God was their main focus. To them, their wealth was not their life, but their relationship with God was the center of their life. Likewise, wealth should never be our life's focus since it is just a part of life; it is not life itself. Wealth should never come in between the person's life and Christ. The relationship with God should be first and foremost and should be nurtured whether rich or poor, just like Job and Abraham did. Job's children and wealth, for instance, were taken away, and yet he believed and trusted in God. As a result, God gave him more wealth than what he originally had. God alone can make our life happy and abundant.

God alone can make our life happy and abundant.

I shall also add that wealth is a blessing that should be shared and not hoarded. Those who have wealth should have a greater responsibility to help the needy or to tackle the world's problem of hunger and poverty. It should be an opportunity since the result of sharing and helping is joy and fulfillment. When children share their toys with other children, for instance, the parents are proud and happy. They usually complement their children for their admirable character of sharing. Likewise, when a person gives to the needy, he or she is making the Provider feel proud. God expects His children to honor Him by using the wealth that they have to bless others. A beautiful movie some of you might have seen is the Schindler's List. A war story about a businessman who saved many Jews by employing them in his factory. At the end of the war, he cried realizing he could have saved more Jews by selling his belongings, by not spending unnecessarily, and if he could have only made more money.

There are some who pretend to be rich but have nothing, and some pretend to be poor but have great wealth (Proverbs 13:7). Unknown to most people, Mother Teresa lived a life of abundance and contentment. She is one of the paragons of rich in life without having wealth. It was known that she only had three pairs of clothes, one that she had on, one that was about to be washed, and a clean one about to be worn. She devoted her life to serving the needy children in India and other countries. I once heard a speaker who had the opportunity to meet Mother Teresa in person talk about her once. When they met, she asked Mother Teresa, "What can I do to help you?" Mother Teresa replied, "My child, do you have a family?" She said, "Yes, I do." Mother Teresa then said, "My child, go home to your family and take care of them and love them." Mother Teresa knew that love in God and family is the most important in life. Loving relationships and contentment and not wealth is the core of abundant life, as we shall see in the next chapters.

CHAPTER 10

CONTENTMENT AND
ABUNDANT LIFE

As illustrated by Mother Theresa, contentment cannot be undermined, for it is one of the important keys to abundant living. It is a remedy for greed or for those who focus their life on accumulating wealth. It is a rare gift that only a few are blessed with. It is a great treasure that everyone should acquire because it is one of the elements to right living.

Contentment may sound easy, but it is actually difficult for many to do. Even some of God's children have some difficulty achieving contentment. Here is some wisdom from other people who understand the value of contentment:

> Contentment is a pearl of great price, and whoever procures it at the expense of ten thousand desires makes a wise and a happy purchase.[8]

> There is no end of craving. Hence contentment alone is the best way to happiness. Therefore, acquire contentment.[9]

> Man falls from the pursuit of the ideal of plan living and high thinking the moment he wants to

multiply his daily wants. Man's happiness really lies in contentment.[10]

One of the secrets to happiness is the ability to be content.

It is true that one of the secrets to happiness is the ability to be content. But most of us do not know how to be content because the media, our cultures, our friends and relatives, or our surroundings have created in us the abnormal desire and the need for power, prestige, money, possessions, and beauty that only create stress, anxiety, and tension. Some are not contented with their breasts, nose, lips, or entire body. A dark-skinned woman, for instance, would want a lighter skin, and the light-skinned woman would want a darker skin. A curly-haired woman would want a straight hair, and the straight-haired woman would want a curly hair. Many are not happy because they fail to recognize that the root of their misery is not because of what they don't have but due to covetousness, jealousy, pride, greed, ungratefulness, and unfulfilled expectations.

We are lying when we say that we are content and yet we covet our neighbor's bigger house, better car, bigger television, their beautiful wife, and so on. Our pride is so high we have to have a better, bigger, or more expensive stuff than our neighbors, friends, or siblings. We buy things just to impress others. Unknowingly, sometimes our discontent draws us into troublesome ways of thinking and living. Jomich, for instance, wanted a 75-inch television because his neighbor has a 50-inch television. But Jomich had a dilemma because now his neighbor bought a bigger TV that's mounted on his wall with a surround sound system. (See, I just mentioned the TV with surround sound, and some of you already want to run and go get one). But now Jomich is not happy, and what's worse, he now despises his neighbor without his neighbor knowing it. He even has a bigger dilemma since his children are pressuring him to buy the same things. But, folks, believe it or not this is a big problem. We want what others have and we are not going to be happy not until we get it. Many of us are in debt by being in this situation. Sometimes, we are blinded by the reality that these dilemmas could destroy relationships and families.

Nowadays it is even more difficult to be content because of media and advertising. The media makes us think and feel that a bigger house, a fancier car, or a bigger TV with surround sound will make us happy. They make us think that Barbie doll bodies are the norm, while in fact, only a few young women have them. Moreover, we believe the media and allow it to dictate our likes and dislikes. Many are in a trance following what it shows, and what's worse, we believe its contents. We neglect or fail to recognize that media are there to make money, and that money comes from the consumers who buy whatever they dish out.

Furthermore, the media rarely state the side effects of what you buy. A few, like the medical products, mentions the side effects, but they say it so fast or make the label so small it makes the side effects sound or look irrelevant. But if you listen carefully and really digest what they say it does to your bodies and brains, you will perhaps not buy the product or find an alternative. They also do not tell you the bad effect of having bigger TV. They do not warn you that a bigger

TV could rob you of quality time that could have been spent with your family or neighbor. It could, for instance, ruin your eardrum, your eyes, or worse, your brain. Yes, it could ruin your brain because they are very good at making you believe at what they say, while in fact, most of what they show are sensationalized and just for entertainment; after all, that's what they are—the entertainment industry. It is about impressing and blowing your mind out. Most of what they dish out could devalue your brain.

But if we stop watching TV programs that could stall our intelligence, then perhaps we could at least learn how to spend our time and money wisely and perpetuate more contentment and less covetousness. If we instill some sense of control to recognize media's deceptions, then we could at least save a part of our brain. Most of us are oblivious to the fact that the media is one of the architects or mastermind of covetousness. The media teaches us how to covet by enticing us with their products and services. If we are aware about this and realize that we are breaking God's tenth commandment when we are doing it, then perhaps we will learn how to be content. God said, "You shall not covet your neighbor's house; you shall not covet your neighbor's wife or his male servant or his female servant or his ox or his donkey [his car] or anything that belongs to your neighbor's" (Exodus 20:17). When we reach the point of not coveting our neighbors' stuff, then we have achieved contentment. But if we find ourselves wanting more and more, then we need to figure out the root of our discontent.

Discontent and our demanding spirit make us unhappy, and it make our lives miserable and causes us to sin more and more. One of the causes of discontent is greed. Greed is bad news because it breeds greedy people. We are greedy when instead of giving to the poor we trade our new Toyota Camry with a new Lexus. Discontent is trading our three-bedroom house into a five-bedroom house even though in reality we only need three since there are only two in the family. We claim that we need more room because we buy stuff that don't fit in our house. We accumulate too much stuff that we don't need. We need to realize that bigger and better stuff will never make us content. But if we pile up treasures in heaven by helping the needy, then not only do we make our life better but the lives of the needy as well. There are many people who need help, and some of them are our close relatives.

I have a friend in Belgium who worked as a caregiver for a long time just to be able to send to college her sisters and brothers in the Philippines. She was not happy with her job, but she had to endure to help her family back home. I cried with tears of compassion listening to her sacrifices just to help her family. I asked if any of her brothers or sisters finished school, and she happily and proudly said yes. She said one of her sisters became a lawyer. And recently, the lawyer volunteered to pay for her airfare to visit home. I said, "Wow, what an awesome story! No wonder you are very motivated to help your family."

I asked another friend of mine in Belgium, named Anita, to give me her definition of abundant life. She said, "For me, abundant life is when my needs and wants are fulfilled." I asked her if she is having an abundant life using her definition, and she said yes and no. I asked her to explain. She said, "My life is not completely abundant because I often think of my relatives in the Philippines whose lives are not abundant." She works as a chambermaid at a hotel, but she is able to experience abundance through contentment and by helping her family in the Philippines.

Most of us do not realize that we have a lot of wealth, but we use these riches to satisfy our greed, neglecting those who are in need. We do not realize that the true wealth is not what we have but what we do to others. We were not made to hoard for ourselves; we were made to share and help others. One should be inspired to help those in need since helping always brings joy to both the receiver and the giver. Moreover, helping someone without anyone knowing gives us some sense of joy, self-fulfillment, revitalized life, and honor.

My coworker who was in the hospital needed some sick leave donation so she could continue to get paid while in the hospital. I was looking at my accumulated sick time and thought that I could afford to donate forty hours (five days or one week) of sick leave. This was a difficult decision since we accumulate eight hours per month. That means, I worked five months to gain forty hours. I started thinking that I should donate twenty-four hours of sick time so she could at least have three more days of sick leave with pay. In my mind, that was what she deserved since she offended me one time, and I heard some negative information about her. Then I changed my mind and added one more day. I completed the form, putting in thirty-two hours, but did not submit it. I went home, and God taught me a lesson the next day about grace. God blesses the just and the unjust—that is grace. He does not look at us or judge us if we deserve grace; He gives it anyway. So I changed the form and donated a week of sick leave to my coworker because of what I learned from God.

Ungratefulness is another cause of discontent. Most of us are blessed with wealth and possessions beyond our needs, but we often-times do not recognize this blessing. As mentioned previously, we do not recognize these awesome gifts because we are too caught up with keeping up with the Joneses, and we are too greedy to know it. We are blinded by our greed and discontent that we fail to thank the Almighty for the blessings that He has provided. We fail to thank Him for the food, for the shelter, for the clothing, and for the healthy body that we enjoy. We fail to recognize that we are eating good food compared to the poor children in other countries. We fail to be thankful for the small house that keep us from heat and cold while there are many others who are homeless. We fail to recognize that we may have a small house with one TV and one living room but the whole family gets to happily enjoy watching television together, and what's more, the communication and relationship is better. With a bigger house, everyone disappears to his or her own hub, watches TV in their own rooms, and good communication is gone. Moreover, keeping up with the Joneses is oftentimes a bad example to our children, and we become bad, instead of wise, consumers. We teach our children to be grateful and be content, but we ourselves are ungrateful and discontent.

Ungratefulness to our parents is I think the greatest deficiency in our society today. Some children disrespect and treat their parents like nobodies. They are ungrateful to the one who took good care of them when they could not take care of themselves. They are ungrateful to the one who provided for their needs, bought their clothes, cooked their food, and cleaned their house. They are ungrateful to the parents who want nothing but the best for them. Every normal parent wants their children to grow and have better lives than what they had. They want their children to be better parents, doctors, lawyers, or citizens. Almost all parents love their children deeply that they try their best to raise them with tender, loving care or the best that they could. They try to provide for their wants and needs as much as they can. But. some children are ungrateful and do not recognize this love. that's probably why Mother's Day and Father's Day were created, perhaps to remind us that we have parents who are special, and we should thank them for their love and guidance. Ungratefulness to our parents is one of the greatest sins because we are commanded to honor our father and mother; it is the fifth commandment.

One should learn from grateful people, for they are the ones who can demonstrate a life full of contentment. They are most thankful and most appreciative with anything that they have whether big or small, cheap or expensive. They are humble and are contented whether they are rich or poor. They do not focus on what they don't have but on what they have. Even if they are poor, they feel that they are rich and are showered with blessings bountifully. They would say something like, "I don't know why God has blessed me so much. I surely do not deserve it, but I am very, very grateful." They feel that they do not deserve all this, and so they are exceedingly grateful for what they have. They know too well the secret and the joy of giving, and so they look for opportunities to help and share their blessings. Sometimes, they even sacrifice their own needs just to help someone in great need.

When we recognize the root of our discontent and learn to be content, life is more fulfilling, we are at peace, and we are at rest. We avoid anxiety, stress, and tension, which make our life more complicated than it already is. Contentment is being satisfied with the state we are in, but we are to continue to seek the pearls of wisdom and knowledge. Perhaps there are other roots of discontent that are not mentioned here; recognize or identify them and then delete them. Throw away false reasoning that causes discontent or every thought that keeps us from being content. If we focus our energy in building treasures in heaven, we will gain contentment and the true joy that it brings.

CHAPTER 11

BUILDING TREASURES IN HEAVEN

The quality of our decisions could bring about positive outcomes not only in our life but in the lives of others as well. Bringing our decisions to a higher ground, for instance, accelerating our human potential to a higher level, such as acquiring contentment, loving the unlovable, controlling our anger, and forgiving our offender, could open ourselves up to greater possibilities and opportunities of true human goodness and joy. The more we decide to bring about goodness to our decisions, such as building treasures in heaven, the better character we develop in our life and the life of others.

The treasures that I've been talking about are unlike the treasure we have on earth. It is not money, gold, or diamonds. The treasures are admirable characters we need to develop in order to live in God's kingdom here on earth and perhaps in heaven someday. They are noble characters or virtuous qualities that we develop to give value to our life and the life of others. Unlike treasures in heaven, treasures on earth do not have heavenly value. It can be traded, sold, or disposed of easily. Treasures in heaven, on the other hand, are valuable and cannot be traded or sold since it is priceless. It benefits not only the person accumulating the wealth but others as well.

There are many big treasures that one can accumulate such as obedience to God and freedom from having to sin. But let us explore other already mentioned valuable treasures, such as loving the unlovable, loving our enemies, controlling our anger, and forgiving our offenders, that are important jewels for abundant life. These are precious and priceless treasures because they are valuable for life. Jesus said, "Do not store up for yourselves treasures on earth, where thieves break in and steal; but store up for yourselves treasures in heaven, where neither moth nor rust consumes and where thieves do not break in and steal" (Matthew 6:19–20)." Financial wealth will stay here on earth when a person dies. Character wealth, on the other hand, will benefit the person and others not only here on earth but in heaven as well.

However, piling up this kind of treasures is sometimes difficult, and it takes time, energy, and effort. As said earlier, we will be living in heaven someday, so we should know how to act as children of God here on earth. But for many, living in God's kingdom takes a lot of work. It is not easy. God said, "You can enter God's Kingdom only through the narrow gate. The highway to hell is broad, and its gate is wide for the many who choose the easy way. But the gateway to life is small and the road is narrow, and only a few ever find it" (Matthew 7:13–14). A rich young ruler came to Jesus to inquire about obtaining eternal life, saying, "What good thing shall I do that I may obtain eternal life?" Jesus responded by enumerating some of the basics of the Ten Commandments:

> "You shall not commit murder; You shall not commit adultery; You shall not steal; You shall not bear false witness; Honor your father and mother; and you shall love your neighbor as yourself." The young ruler replied, "All these things I have kept, what am I still lacking?" Jesus then replied, "If you wish to be complete, go sell your possessions and give to the poor, and you shall have treasure in heaven; and come follow Me." But when the young man heard this statement, he went away grieved; for he was one who owned much property. (Matthew 19:16–26)

Piling up treasures in heaven is oftentimes difficult since it could take a life-changing event. In fact, it's almost impossible, but again it can be done though Christ and with the Holy Spirit as our Helper. Jesus said, "With man this is impossible, but with God all things are possible" (Matthew 19:26).

Allow me to illustrate some jewels that could help us get closer to heaven and that will certainly change our life for the better. My favorite and the largest jewel is *love*.

The Excellence of Love

I heard many definitions of love since I was a teenager. Some of these were: "Love is a many splendored thing," "Love is blind," "Love is what you make out of it," etc. Even the Greeks categorize and define love in different ways. But the real definition of love, in my opinion, comes from the biblical text. Here is a biblical illustration of what I find to be the demonstration of the excellence of love:

> If I speak the languages of men and of angels but do not have love,
>
> I am a sounding gong or a clanging cymbal.
>
> If I have the gift of prophecy, and understand all mysteries and all knowledge, and if I have all faith so that I can move mountains but do not have love, I am nothing.
>
> And if I donate all my goods to feed the poor, and if I give my body to be burned, but do not have love I gain nothing.
>
> Love is patient; love is kind.
>
> Love does not envy; is not boastful; is not conceited; does not act improperly; is not selfish; is not provoked; does not keep a record of wrongs; finds no joy in unrighteousness, but

rejoices in the truth; bears all things, believes all
things, hopes all things, endures all things.
Love will never end. (1 Corinthians 13)

The above masterpiece is, in my opinion, the ideal, the model,
and the paragon of love. Paul said, "Now these three remain: faith,
hope and love. But the greatest of these is love (1 Corinthians 13:13)."
Now why do you think Paul makes love the best or highest of all? I
think it is because *love* is a mighty and powerful jewel that can change
a person, a country, and the world. It has been known that love could
launch a thousand ships and could tame the beast. But it is a reality that it is through love that humans are conceived, and the earth
created. It is through love that brought God's Son into this world. It
is through love that we become one with one another beyond skin
colors. It is the reason why we connect and bond with one another.
It is the only thing that infiltrates socio-cultural boundaries. Love
determines the essence of our existence, and it knows no bounds. It
makes us happy, sad, and angry and gives a reason to smile and live.
Believe it or not, love is the reason why we are alive. It is the reason
why we haven't killed one another. It is the reason we are patient and
kind to our children and the reason we are able to forgive. It is the
reason why we cry and grieve when we lose someone. Love is the only
powerful change agent that produces positive results.

The above definition also tells me that if I keep record of my
husband's faults and if I am not patient and kind to my children, then
I fall short of the excellence of love. I had a dilemma once because
one of my greatest skills was keeping records of wrong things that my
loved ones, my relatives, and my friends did or do. I did not keep a
written list, but I had a detailed mental list of every mistake or wrong
in my brain—and it was long. However, for some reason, I had a
short list hidden in my memory of the good things that they have
done, and oftentimes this list remained hidden. The bad list could
easily be pulled up than the good list, and what's more, it would con-
veniently resurface when arguments arise. Most of you are perhaps
the same way. You probably use the bad list to remind your loved

ones of the wrong things they have done. You probably use these as darts, seeing which ones hit the bull's eye.

It took a while before I realized that this was actually a bad skill since it just hurt the ones I love. So I decided to purge the list from my brain. I thought it would make not my life but the life of my love one's better. But I soon found out that it was difficult to erase them because they were embedded in my memory. And so I just had to learn to bite my tongue whenever this list would come out and not bring it out during heated discussions. This usually took conscious effort and energy since I was used to saying anything in my mind. It is usually difficult to bite our tongue and choose not to bring the past back. This is important because most of us do make mistakes that we often regret. But these mistakes can stay on in our lives forever because someone—and oftentimes that someone is very close to us—makes sure that we do not forget what we did. That someone is notorious at continuously making our lives miserable by bringing the same mistake over and over again whenever they have the opportunity. Humans are not immune to making bad choices. We just hope that our loved ones are still there once we come to our senses and realize our mistake.

A man made a serious mistake of dating another woman while going steady with a beautiful woman named Katelyn. When Katelyn found out about it, she ended their relationship right away. But for some reason, there was this mysterious, powerful force called love that brought them back together again. However, after they got married, Katelyn would always use this mistake as a weapon to get what she wanted, to win an argument, to shut him up, or to pierce his heart. Unknown to him, his mistake had left a big scar within her that was difficult to ignore, which is why it would automatically come out in an argument. The husband took the beatings for many years until Katelyn learned to dump this weapon.

I would like to stress that oftentimes the very ones we love are the ones we hurt the most. Hence, we must learn not to use any weapon that hurt, and usually if we get rid of it, oftentimes it actually stays hidden and, at its best, gone. The definition of love previously stated expects us not to keep a record of wrongs, to be kind, to bear all things, to not act improperly, and to be not provoked. Relationship is much better when it is nurtured with forgiveness, kindness, and love. Life is easier if the goal is to live in harmony with others.

Love should always build up and not destroy; it should understand, and it should be redemptive. Love is a verb that requires action, but a positive and sometimes a negative action. If a child steals money, for instance, the positive thing that one can do is to make the child apologize and return the money. But a negative response could be to institute what we call tough love, or punish the child, to ensure that this situation will not happen again.

Tough love oftentimes takes energy and is difficult to apply, but the end result makes us proud and happy. We want the best for our loved ones, but sometimes it is difficult to love or to remain rational when our emotions are running high. Regardless, the purpose of tough love should be to save a person from evil, to break someone of stubborn will, or to lead someone to maturity and not injury. The intention should be to instill a lesson that results into an admirable character.

Sometimes we say or do things that we don't mean, not knowing that we could leave an unpleasant scar that stays forever. We seldom think before we say things and perhaps rationalize on how the words that come out of our mouth affect others. What we say should edify and build instead of destroy. Relationships could be difficult if the persons involved destroy each other instead of loving and respecting one another. It is easier to get angry and counter the person who is doing us wrong with another wrong, paying evil for evil. To some, it is even more difficult to stay calm and think and counter bad for good or repay good for evil. Why is it difficult? It is hard because we are used to it, it is embedded as a habit, or we have been trained well for it. Some of us were never trained to counter good for evil. The Bible, however, teaches and encourages us to love our enemies. In Proverbs 21:21, it says, "Whoever pursues godliness and unfailing love will find life, godliness and honor."

"Whoever pursues godliness and unfailing love will find life, godliness and honor." Proverbs 21:21

Human love is oftentimes self-serving, conditional, and selfish; we always want something in return for something. When we love, we expect better love in return. When we give something, we expect a bigger and better, something like profit, in return, whether now or in the future. Even when we donate to churches, some of us expect and hope for a seat in heaven. But is it possible to love and give and not expect anything in return? Is it possible to love our enemy and not expect them to love us back? Yes, it is possible. God's love is not selfish, is not self-serving, and is not conditional. God demonstrated his love toward us in that while we were still sinners, Christ died for us (Romans 5:8). God is the author of love because He is love. And when we have the Holy Spirit living in us, we are able to love like God. God gave us and showed us the paragon of love so we can love others unconditionally. When a man asked Jesus what the greatest commandment is, He said, "You shall love the LORD your God with all your heart, with all your soul, and with all your mind. This is the first and great commandment. And the second is like it: You shall love your neighbor as yourself" (Matthew 22:37–39). This commandment is clear—we are to love our God, friends and relatives or our neighbors unconditionally.

The excellence of love suggests that I may have everything in the world but if I have not loved, then I am nothing. I would like to expound this definition in simpler terms. What do we gain if we have all the wealth and knowledge in this world, but we are selfish, unforgiving, and conceited? What do we gain if we are a good preacher and have all faith and know all the Holy Scriptures if we are insensitive and unkind to the needy or if we mistreat our spouse and children? And what do we gain if we feed the poor and help the needy if we are dishonest and we cheat our family and others and if we discriminate and despise others? What do we gain if we have everything but we rob our family and the people around us of the love they deserve?

Love is more meaningful if we love the unlovable, if we forgive the unforgiveable, if we give till it hurts, if we turn the other cheek, if preachers (and everyone) practice what they preach, if we do not keep grudges, and if we never give up on someone. The excellence of love is demonstrated when we give others the worth that they deserve. It is demonstrated when we love unconditionally, when we are patient and kind, and when we help build them up to the best they can be. Love covers a multitude of sins. Perfect love casts out evil, and love and righteousness reigns. Love is the most expensive and the most powerful jewel because it gives significance and value to life.

Love the Unlovable

One way of placing ourselves in the service of love is loving the unlovable. My husband had a fortune cookie hidden in his wallet for quite some time until I took it and lost it. It said, "The best way to defeat your enemy is to make him your friend." Now I know this is difficult to do because I have experienced it. It is difficult to love our enemies. Be impressive sometime and impress yourself and others by loving your enemy. There is no challenge in loving those who love us.

I had a co-worker once who was unlovable because she was harsh, mean, impossible, and she always got her way through intimidation. One day, I was mad at what she did that I finally thought, "Well, there's no use confronting her because she will just be harsh and splatter my words back to my face. So this time I will try not my way but God's way." I decided to add a jewel in heaven by gathering some courage and energy to pray for blessings for my enemy. I said, "Lord, you said to pray for your enemies, so I am praying for [her name]. Bless her, Lord, because she really needs it. Please shower your blessings on her. Love her, Lord, and comfort her and provide for her." It was difficult for me to pray blessings for her, but I had to try God's way. I was reminded of the verses in the Bible. In Matthew 5:44, it says, "But I say, love your enemies! Pray for those who persecute you!" In Colossians 3:13, it says, "You must make allowance for each other's faults and forgive the person who offends you. Remember, the Lord forgave you, so you must forgive others." Because of these commands, I did not only pray for her, but I also greeted her with a smile from the Lord—yes, a smile from the Lord because it was difficult for me to smile at her naturally. But God gave me the strength to do the right thing—to love my enemy.

After I continually prayed for her, I was very amazed at the result. My attitude toward her changed, and her attitude toward me changed as well. She started being nice by giving me gifts, building me up to our boss, giving me sound advice, etc. I said to myself, "Wow! This is so good I can do this again and again." Instead of letting her ruin my life, by obeying God, she made my life better and happier. It works! I tried it, and not only did it make my world a better place, but I also added a jewel to my treasure in heaven.

> Do not repay anyone evil for evil. Try to do what is honorable in everyone's eyes. If possible, on your part, live at peace with everyone. Friends, do not avenge yourselves; instead, leave room for His wrath. For it is written; Vengeance belongs to me; I will repay, says the Lord, but if your enemy is hungry, feed him. If he is thirsty, give him something to drink. For in so doing you will be heaping fiery coals on his head. Do not be conquered by evil, but conquer evil with good. (Romans 12:17–21)

> But if you are willing to listen, I say, love your enemies. Do good to those who hate you. Pray for happiness of those who curse you. Pray for those who hurt you. If someone slaps you on one cheek, turn the other cheek. If someone demands your coat, offer your shirt also… Do to others as you would like them to do for you. (Luke 6:27–31)

There is no peace or joy in paying evil for evil. Life is more peaceful if we pay good for evil, what's more, goodness will increase and evil will decrease. The Bible says, "When a man's ways please the Lord, He makes even his enemies to be at peace with him" (Proverbs 16:7).

Controlling Anger

Another jewel that we could add to our treasure in heaven is restraining from anger. Anger is a natural reaction that gains nothing but lose everything instead. It is not good since the reaction could result in injury or death. It is a powerful emotion that could hurt. Some people have a difficult time restraining anger because they are not trained to control this kind of emotion. I, for instance, get easily angry when I see abuse or when someone cuts me off in line or on the road especially when I am in a hurry. In these situations, it is hard to first calm down and think of a positive response. We usually just let it out and let anger control us instead of us controlling our anger. Since anger comes naturally, it is difficult to use some good sense and perhaps think and say something like, "Maybe he is in more of a hurry than I am because his wife is having a baby, or he is on his way to the hospital or worst he has to use the bathroom!"

Anger can cloud our judgement and can also lead to danger. Someone once said, "Anger is one letter away from danger." It is a reality that anger could hurt you or the person around you. There are many situations where anger has led to death. I previously stayed at a center for battered women, and I remember meeting many abused women from all walks of life. I remember a woman who killed her husband because of being fed up with the abuse. I remember some men hurting their wives because of uncontrolled emotions. I also learned that abuse is a choice, and a man can choose not to get angry and hurt his wife.

Anger can darken our hearts and can lead us to do things that we would never do or say when our emotions are unstable. Our heart is darkened when we allow anger to control our emotion that could potentially hurt someone. One of the cruelest mistreatment that I have ever witnessed while I was at the abuse center was a woman who had iron marks all over her body. Her angry husband burned her body with hot iron, leaving iron-shaped imprints all over. Darkened hearts do dark actions with dark consequences that are sometimes irreversible.

Although anger is natural to mankind, all of us can master our anger by choosing not to let our emotion go wild. Oftentimes, rage is difficult to control since emotion is running high, and the tendency when one is in this state is to hurt someone, to retaliate, or to get even. At this stage, we usually lose rationality and the reality that "a fool vents his feelings, but a wise man holds them back" (Proverbs 29:11).

Most of us easily get hurt and get angry when someone says unkind words, but we never think of hurting someone when we say the same kind of words. Words are like seeds that could grow inside of us. Positive or good words could sprout and consequently empower us to be better persons. Bad or negative words do not only hurt, but they could destroy us or pull us down and stunt our growth.

Moreover, precious relationships, and sometimes love and our loved ones, cannot be recovered once words that hurt are introduced. It can cause us to distance ourselves from our loved ones and from our God. When we say hurtful words, especially to someone who is close to us, we usually cannot take it back since our harsh words have already penetrated their bones, and it usually hurts the person more than we want or intend it to be. Even if we apologize, the relationship is no longer as warm as it was. The beauty of the relationship is scarred for life.

Hence, in order to avoid such undesirable occasions, we should master how to control anger early in life. Here are some suggestions to remember to help bridle our anger:

- Exercise thinking before talking.
- Pray! Give your anger to God, and don't forget to forgive. Forgiveness restores relationships and mends broken hearts.
- Answer softly, using words that are gentle and soothing. "A soft answer turns away wrath, but a harsh word stirs up anger" (Proverbs 15:1). "A word fitly spoken is like apples of gold in settings of silver" (Proverbs 25:11).

- Be slow to speak and slow to get angry. "He who is slow to wrath has great understanding, but he who is impulsive exalts folly" (Proverbs 14:29).
- Remember, anger does not resolve anything; it just leads to confrontation, resentment, bitterness, and misery.
- Don't expect people to be perfect; give allowance to faults, mistakes, and stupidity.
- Seek out the source of anger, understand the situation, and talk about it.
- Don't try to hold on to rights and expectations that produce anger.
- Isolate anger to the incident itself, and do not take it further, anywhere, anytime, or in the relationship.

There are many benefits of being slow to get angry. Let's try to do this exercise. Imagine yourself in past situations where you were quick to get angry. Now imagine yourself in that similar situation but being slow to get angry, I mean very, very slow, as slow as the slow-motion pictures we see on TV or movies. Does it make a big difference? It should, because being slow to get angry gives you time to think of the appropriate action, what to do or say next. Or perhaps you were too slow that you did not have time to show your anger and your offender had already left. Your offender will probably be back apologizing before you retaliate, and the awesome thing about it is, you are not the one asking for an apology. James, the half-brother of Jesus and who was a leader in Jerusalem church, gave practical advice regarding living a Christian life. With regards to anger he said, "My dear brothers and sisters, be quick to listen, slow to speak, and slow to get angry. Your anger can never make things right in God's sight" (James 1:19, 20).

I remember getting mad at my son for something he did at school during his middle school years. He came home that day telling me to go to his school the next day to talk to his teacher. I inquired what happened, and he explained that someone reported that he had done something wrong. I was so angry with him that I just had to punish him right away, even though he kept insisting that he did not do it. The next day, I went to his school to confirm and apologize for my son's undesirable behavior, only to find out that it was not him. It was someone else's kid who had the same name. I felt shame, for I had already punished my son. I apologized and vowed to myself not to make the same mistake again. "The intelligent person restrains his words, and one who keeps a cool head is a man of understanding. Even a fool is considered wise when he keeps silent, discerning when he seals his lips" (Proverbs 17:27–28).

Another antiserum that we already mentioned is love. Yes, it is possible to love someone even in a state of anger. If a person is able to set aside the rage and communicate the anger openly, yes, it is possible. Married couples, for instance, sometimes war with each other, and yet they allow their love to reign over their anger. They are able to subdue or confine their anger in and around the problem and communicate without provoking the other to anger. They have learned to capitalize on confrontation by showing calmness, dignity, composure, kindness, and love in these situations. They know that "whoever has no rule over his own spirit is like a city broken down without walls" (Proverbs 25:28). They are able to rationalize, they have tamed their feelings, or they have learned the beauty of being slow in anger. Some rare couples use this opportunity to gain more love and respect and to get closer to each other. Because they are able to forgive, they change and get closer by solving their problems in a calm and rational way. They have learned the value of attacking the problem and not each other.

Another popular prescription to anger is choosing not to let it affect your life. Someone once said, "Self-sacrifice through self-control is necessary for self-fulfillment." You can always choose not to get angry and chose to have joy instead. If, for instance, someone upsets you, chose the high road and give allowance to your transgressor, and chose to be calm and happy instead. After all, "A joyful heart is good medicine, but a broken spirit dries up the bones" (Proverbs 17:22). If things don't go your way, do not be uptight about it since it just adds wrinkles to your face. Don't allow anyone to rob you of your daily joy by giving way to anger. I knew someone who wasted many years of inner peace because she allowed bitterness to steal her joy. Consequently, it's our choice; either we count it all joy and have life or let anger and misery consume our sunny life.

Forgiveness

Another precious jewel that we can deposit in heaven is forgiving our offenders. Forgiving leads to a peaceful life, and as just said, it restores relationships and mends broken hearts. As long as we have hatred in our hearts, we will never have peace. This is a very important decision because without forgiveness, a person will live in misery, anger, and bitterness. Living in this condition can rob a person of abundant life. That's why Our Creator commands us to forgive and love our enemies because the end result is for our well-being and the well-being of others. It is obvious that if we love and forgive someone, we are not going to do anything to hurt that person. That's why Christ made forgiveness a prerequisite to receiving God's forgiveness. In Matthew 18:35, God said, "Forgive and you will be forgiven." Moreover, in Ephesians 4, God said,

> Be angry, and do not sin. Do not let the sun go down on your wrath, nor give place to the devil… Let all bitterness, wrath, anger, clamor, and evil speaking be put away from you, with all malice. Be kind to one another, tenderhearted, forgiving, one another, even as God in Christ forgave you. (Ephesians 4:26–27, 31–32)

God wants us to forgive because He knows that if we don't, we will be living in pain and festering anger, and this awful feeling more often than not makes our lives miserable because it eats away our inner being. What's more, staying in this condition could affect others as well. We sulk and brood and look in despair, contaminating others. Bitterness is Satan's way of making us look bad. Some of us do not realize it, but this bitterness shows in our face, in the way we talk, and in our words. We look scary and angry, and we utter unpleasant words. Many avoid this kind of people because they do not usually listen, they are always negative, and they can become the enemy without doing or saying anything. Do not give way to Satan's device and deception. Defeat Satan by forgiving your enemy. Do not allow Satan to ruin your inner peace, depriving you of a peaceful life.

Bitterness can create physical illnesses as well. A person can sometimes have high blood pressure, headaches, body aches, or even be depressed. It is an unpleasant feeling to allow anger or hurt feelings dwell in our life. That's why in Hebrews 12, God said, "Pursue peace with all people, and holiness, without which no one will see the Lord." God gave this command because it is not only good for our physical and mental health but for our spiritual well-being as well. For this reason, a real and genuine change in our attitude and in our way of life is needed to overcome bitterness. An inner transformation or overhaul is needed to forgive and clean away the crud inside us, which slowly chokes away our happy life.

One Sunday, our pastor's wife spoke about forgiveness, and she said, "Bitterness could be like an acorn that falls to the ground in a beautiful garden. It sprouts and grows into a small tiny tree, and if it's not pulled from the ground, it will grow and grow and grow into a tree. The longer you wait, the harder it is to pull it out of the ground. If you let it grow to become a tree, it will overshadow your garden, just like bitterness can overshadow or rule your life." This story is relevant because we can decide and chose to forgive and let it go or let bitterness rule our life, causing anger and misery. Folks, if it is hard to forgive someone—ask God to help you forgive.

According to the Internet, the definition of *forgiveness* is "the mental, emotional and/or spiritual process of ceasing to feel resentment or anger against another person for a perceived offence, difference or mistake, or ceasing to demand punishment or restitution." Forgiveness transcends all offenses big or small; it ends resentment and anger toward another. It is an act of humility that restores relationships. By choosing to forgive, we will develop character, we will experience freedom from bitterness, we will build treasures in heaven, and we will have abundant life. Yes, the feeling of being free from sin, from hating your enemy, and from bitterness that eats away our abundant life is much better than being angry, sad, and bitter. God said, "And don't sin by letting anger gain control over you. Don't let the sun go down while you are still angry, for anger gives a mighty foothold to the Devil." He also said, "See that no one pays back evil for evil, but always try to do good to each other and to everyone else" (1 Thessalonians 5:15). This command is clear. Not only are we to forgive our offenders, but we should always seek what is good for one another. Forgiving results in freedom from something that carries heavy in the heart. Forgiving removes the root and the source of bitterness that ruins happy life and precious relationships. Forgiving spares lives and encourages reconciliation. It builds relationship, promotes peace, and guess what? Love reigns.

Piling up treasures in heaven could be difficult since it takes energy and effort, but it could also be fun and fulfilling. It is difficult and challenging but rewarding as well. The important thing is that the end result is always positive. By loving our enemies, we become peacemakers, and if you do not know it yet, Jesus loves the peacemakers. He said, "Blessed are the peacemakers because they will be called sons of God" (Matthew 5:9). And by forgiving our enemies, we heal broken hearts, we restore relationships and fellowship, and we improve not only our well-being but the well-being of others as well. Ultimately, our decisions to love unconditionally, to love the unlovable, to restrain from anger, and to forgive our offenders, these are the real treasures of heaven and of life.

CHAPTER 12

A MEANINGFUL LIFE

Now you may ask, what is a meaningful life? You may have noticed that I have answered this question in previous chapters, but why don't you stop reading this book for a while and ask yourself the same question. What is life that has meaning that's fulfilling, and worth living? Am I living a meaningful life? Or better yet, what is the purpose of my life?

I hope you came up with an answer that is more meaningful than mine. To me, life is more meaningful if a person finds out the fundamental truth about the purpose of life. The central foundation of life is living the life that the creator of life intends for us to live; and that is to live a sin-free life, to prosper, and to have an abundant relationship with God and men. Our life is designed to have relationships, whether it's a sisterly, brotherly, friendly, parental or marital relationship. It is our primary purpose in life. Unknown to many, it is where the true wealth of life lies. We were created to need someone, to belong, to interact, or to have companion. The fundamental key to abundant living is based on relationships. That's the reason why God created Adam and Eve.

The saying no man is an island is true. Studies have shown that people in a loving relationship are more likely to be healthier, happier, and more satisfied. Hence, as relational beings, we should be focused on creating relationships that are meaningful, lasting, and valuable. We should be busy in making our relationship work instead of being busy accumulating wealth. We should use our energy in building relationships instead of spending our time ruining it. Relationships are invaluable; it is priceless. Loving relationship with God and men should be the main goal of our living since it is the main purpose of our existence.

If building relationships is everyone's main objective in life, then this world can be in a higher moral ground. There would hardly be any crime since the main focus is the well-being of the other. Relationships should thrive on love, kindness, forgiveness, and care. But if, for instance, our main focus is accumulating wealth, then relationships would be like what we all see in the media today. It is all about self, corruption, greed, cheating, stealing, lying, selfishness, and uncaring lifestyle.

We all know that relationships could fall apart when our focus is immoral. It could fail because we do not understand what constitutes a happy and meaningful relationship. Relationships are made because of a connection; and healthy, happy, and successful relationships work because of nurturing the connection.

A relationship is like a tree, it needs strong roots to nourish itself and to stand firm on the ground. The connection then in relationships is just like the roots of a tree. The roots in relationships, such as love, patience, respect, understanding, forgiveness, and kindness, are relevant; without which, there is no relationship.

I would like to think that the most important root in a relationship is the biggest and strongest root, and that is love. Once this root is damaged, the relationship becomes faulty and is in danger of becoming permanently separated. This root, in my opinion, is the most important since it holds the tree in place; it is the bond that keeps the relationship going. It is a vital connection because once severed, it is difficult to put it back, just like a broken egg.

Some relationships are like eggs; once it is broken, it is difficult or impossible to put it back. But some are like a broken vase; it can be glued back together, and you can't even tell it's broken. Some are like iron pots—it can go through many beatings, but it is only dented;

nothing can break it. Like iron pot, a tree with strong foundation can withstand stress, such as strong winds, floods, or tornadoes.

Relationships are made because of a connection, and a healthy, happy, and successful relationships work because of nurturing the connection.

Hence, in order for relationships to be strong, the roots need to go deep and be given extra love and care. Some of the relevant connections we already mentioned and explained are love, forgiveness, and restraining from anger. Other roots are as important, such as:

- *Respect.* Some teenagers would argue that this is the most important element in a relationship since it gives a person worth, value, honor, and esteem. It is relevant because it deters conflict, and it makes a person feel better.
- *Honesty and trust.* The old saying that honesty is the best policy is true since this is oftentimes the glue to a relationship. But lying or cheating could easily unglue it. Lies have the power to disconnect a relationship, even if one never finds out about the lie. Oftentimes the lie comes

out regardless; it has its way of manifesting mysteriously. Moreover, some of us are transparent when we lie. We feel guilty, uneasy, and constrained. Hence, we should always remember that honesty could save a relationship, but lying could break it permanently.

- *Good communication.* Part of having a good, healthy relationship is enjoying the company of each other. But for this to happen, we should be able to enjoy listening as well as talking to the other person. However, most of us enjoy talking more than listening. We seem to have forgotten that we are created with two ears and one mouth. There is more peace in a relationship when one is willing to listen. But I also want to add that good communication in the midst of a heated discussion can be managed by (a) handling negative feeling that could become undesirable by agreeing a time to talk about it when parties have calmed down—the tongue could be the deadliest and meanest weapon, (b) not criticizing each other—unprofitable talk will do you no good, (c) staying with the topic and avoiding attacking the person, and (d) and by not holding grudges—forgive, forgive, forgive, and forgive.

- *Compromise.* Adversity should not destroy a relationship, but it should bring people together. Many relationships suffer because of our pride, because we fail to forgive, and because we fail to use the beauty of compromise. We always insist on winning or having the last word without realizing that it is more important to maintain a healthy relationship than having the last word and that it is more fun to compromise than argue. I would sometimes pout and raise my voice when my husband and I have an argument, especially when I don't get what I want. He, on the other hand, would just watch me rant and smile and laugh at my pouting and later would sweetly suggest and explain a compromise. Oddly, his compromise is often rational; it makes sense and more objective than mine.

- *Expectations.* Many relationships fail due to expectations that we bring into a relationship. We must remember that no relationship or person is perfect. Sometimes people will frustrate or disappoint each other, and like it or not, this is normal in a relationship. And trying to change our spouses, for instance, to the way we want them to be is not going to work all the time. We might be able to change them, but, in a situation where we cannot, then we should be willing to accept their ways. After all, we want to be at ease when spending time with someone. We should be able to feel good about ourselves and feel comfortable and not be afraid, sad, or worried about our actions. One should enjoy the company instead of feeling pressured to act or to be someone else. Learn how to accept and appreciate differences.

- *Extra mile.* Closeness does not automatically happen in a relationship. It takes work, energy, and going the extra mile to keep the relationship blooming. It is important to make the other person feel special or important, whether it's your husband, friend, child, or parents. Occasionally do something to make the other person feel special, like taking him or her to a movie or to an inexpensive or fine restaurant. One could also buy flowers, chocolate, ice cream or do something simple that he or she likes, something that will put a smile on his or her face. On my way home one day, I bought two scoops of chocolate ice cream on a cone and ran home as fast as I could so the ice cream would not melt. But it started melting, and I started licking while running. Some people were looking at me strangely, and some were smiling. But when I got home and handed my husband his favorite ice cream, he gave me one of the sweetest smiles, and it was all worth it.

- *A healthy relationship is not perfect.* Do not assume that relationships are always perfect. Humans are emotional creatures, with moods and needs that causes contentions.

Recognize that disagreements are a part of human existence, and working through these challenges often makes the relationship better and stronger. Disagreements should be fun to solve; it should not be seen as complications. It should be seen as challenges or an opportunity to solve a complicated situation. It should not be an opportunity to break or hurt a relationship, but an opportunity to get closer, to look into each other's eyes with love and respect and figure a way to solve it. I saw this situation in the movie Overcomer. Such a strong bond of love and respect for each other.

- *The goal in every relationship should be to make the other person happy.* Be a blessing to others. A healthy and happy relationship always find ways to make not just oneself but the other person happy. Be an encourager, a supporter, an unwavering friend. Most of us have perhaps heard the song, "When Mama Ain't Happy." If we make someone happy, it usually has its way of bouncing back with even more satisfying results.

The difference between a happy, fruitful, profound, and successful relationship and a broken or failed relationship is the failure to work together. The keyword here is *work*. Work is difficult especially to the lazy and uncommitted. Sometimes our emotions overpower our brains or our will power, and we just simply quit. One of the fundamental keys to the commitment is the willingness and the energy that we put to make the relationship healthy. Do we put enough effort into it? Do we focus on loving somebody or loving ourselves alone? Do we tap to our reserve energy and forgive the unforgivable? Do we give up, or are we committed to it no matter what? Most people give up easily because they are hurt, and they fail to allow their brain or good sense or the Holy Spirit to reign over their emotions, or they fail to institute or infuse the reality of love as we have defined earlier. How many times have we regretted what we did because of giving way to our emotions? How many times did we apologize for yelling or saying something unpleasant? How many times have we said to ourselves, "I should have said this or done this instead, but well, it is too late now"?

Sometimes our family and friends abandon us when we shame them or say things when situations are rough and unstable. Instead of being there when they need us the most, we send them out hurting, confused, and we turn our backs on them, not wanting to be associated with the shame or the difficult situation. However, as already mentioned, a person should be a blessing sometime. We should not be takers all the time but givers and sharers of love, care, and kindness. We should be there to encourage or to help stand the already down person.

Investing in a relationship pays off. However, one should also understand that sometimes there are relationships that are not meant to be. No matter how one tries to make it work, it just doesn't flourish. In this situation, it is oftentimes better to let it go before resentment settles in, which could result to unsettling consequences. But every relationship should be worth the sweat. We shouldn't give up because it is hopeless. We may be the only one who can help the person. We may not see the outcome of our hard work; they may change when we die. But loving someone unconditionally and patiently definitely brings about self-fulfillment, satisfying life, and consequently, a meaningful life, just like when one invests into a relationship with Christ.

Relationship with God

Relationship with God is the most important relationship a person will ever have. It is special and fulfilling, more than anyone can imagine. It is not a religion but a personal relationship that is guided by the Holy Spirit. It is a relationship that starts once we allow His Holy Spirit to come into our life so He can take part in our daily lives. If He comes into our life, then our relationship with Christ becomes personal because we become one with Him. This means that God knows everything and anything about us. It means that everything that we are—even all the secrets that our families and friends do not know—God knows it all. He knows all the stealing, cheating, or any vile things that we did or do, and yet He loves us and accepts what we are, who we are, or whatever we have done. This is the awesome beauty of this relationship. It is personal, it is dynamic, it is right, and it is a relationship that is based on love. Christ becomes more than our best friend. He becomes our best friend, our father, our provider, our mentor, our healer, and more. Unlike some of our friends who abandon us when everything gets tough, He is always there for us; He will never leave or quit on us.

Out life was never intended to be without a relationship with our Creator

Our life was never intended to be without a relationship with our Creator. As mentioned earlier, God designed humans to be relational beings. When He fashioned humans, He set aside a part of our being to be void in order for Him to fill. Unknown to many, this void is the part of humanity that seeks for a god. That is the reason why humans like to worship things, whether it is sun, moon, or deities such as Buddha or Zeus. Humanity is designed to hunger for something transcendent. Unfortunately, many do not realize that God is the only transcendent being who can fill this empty space. He wants to fill this void by being involved in our daily life. He said, "Listen! I stand at the door and knock. If anyone hears My voice and opens the door, I will come into him and have dinner with him, and he with Me" (Revelation 3:20).

If we open the door and allow God to come be a part of our daily lives, He will change our life for the better. But if we do not allow Christ to come in, we will never experience the beauty of life that only He can offer. We will miss out on a relationship that is nourished and sustained by the Creator of life. As said early on, without Christ, our life is in darkness—we are living in sin, and we are in a state of hopelessness.

A relationship with Christ should be dynamic and active. It should not be a one-way relationship where we always worship and pray and never know if He answers our prayers or not. We do not even know if He is active in our lives or not. There is a difference between knowing God and experiencing Him, just like there is a difference between knowing Abraham Lincoln and personally knowing him or there is a difference between knowing love and being in love. Similarly, our relationship with Christ should be active. As mentioned early on, His Holy Spirit will live with our spirits generating an interaction. His Spirit lives in us, offering spiritual discernment.

To have discernment, we have to read His Word and talk to God. How do we know what God wants us to do if we do not listen or talk to Him? Praying to a heavenly Father who takes care of our needs, who heals, and who loves us should be the first thing we do in the morning. I don't know about you, but my day is much better when I start my day talking to God. This makes my relationship with God alive and profitable. A relationship is profitable when we obey God's words and promptings, and we see God's provision and active works in our life. When we see God's works in our life, then the relationship becomes stronger and more dynamic because God can take us in areas that we have never been before, and God works in ways that we often do not expect. His works are usually more awesome than what we expect it to be. Abundant life starts when one encounters God and when one is settled internally with God.

While living in California years ago, my husband and I decided to drive to the coast to enjoy the day. However, when we got closer, the coast was cloudy and overcast. The closer we were to the coast, the gloomier it got. There was no sun in sight. But regardless of the cloudy weather, we drove on and settled by the seaside. We took out our chairs, books, and picnic basket to enjoy the scenery. After a while, I decided to walk along the beach just to stretch and to enjoy God's company. I was praising the Lord, talking to Him and asking Him to perhaps show me some of His sense of humor by letting the sun out. After about fifteen to thirty minutes, a hole slowly opened in the sky directly above us, and the sun came out with its radiant rays. It was an awesome sight and an awesome miracle for me to remember the rest of my life. Of course, I was laughing, crying, and praising at the awesomeness of God, just like every time He would do something miraculous like this.

God wants us to enjoy His company and life at its fullest, which is why He created the beautiful earth for us to enjoy. Imagine for a few minutes that there is this king who owns the biggest and richest kingdom in our galaxy who loves you. Because of the king's love for you, he brings you to this beautiful paradise with beautiful flowers, bountiful fruits, clear rivers, majestic trees, and strange creatures to wow you. This paradise is his, but it is given to you so you can explore, live, or do anything with it as you please. He brought you to this awesome place so you can know the depth of his love for you and so you can appreciate him, know him, and get closer to him. All the king wants in return is to have a close relationship with you. But you know humans, we are not always satisfied with anything, so you will probably complain to the king and say, "I love this place, but there is this creature that look like a serpent." So the king sent his son—yes, his son, not his valiant warrior, but his son (since you are very special)—to defeat the serpent for you. He defeated the serpent, but at the cost of the son's life. Understand that this is truly the depth of God's loves for you. You are so special He wants to have a close relationship with you. What would be more awesome than having a close relationship with God. Most of us would be honored and privileged to be Bill Gate's best friend. We would be delighted, proud, and perhaps honored to have a close relationship with the richest man on earth. But God, the Creator and the owner of the earth and everything in it, wants to have a close relationship with you. He is knocking at your door with his arms wide open.

However, this relationship will never grow not until we take some time to get to know our Creator. We will never love a person that we never know. If one truly wants to know or love someone, he or she needs to invest an incredible amount of time to get to know the other. But some would perhaps argue and say something like, "I never knew Brad Pitt personally, but I am in love with him." But the love here is not the "in love" feeling that some women encounter when they see Brad Pitt or James Bond. This kind of love fades and is short-lived. Some couples spend a lot of time together to get to know each other very well before they get married. Normally, the more they know each other and spend time together, the more they draw closer and fall in love. In the same way, we need to spend some time in knowing God to have a personal, meaningful, and dynamic relationship. We need to dig into His life like we are searching for the most valuable treasure on earth. It starts with the person's desire to acquire the Pearl of Great Price. Later, because of the person's zeal, sometimes even with a little effort, the fun journey starts to begin. The Bible is not only the book of life but a book about God as well. We need to dig into Christ's life by reading the Bible, by attending a Bible-believing church, by joining a Bible study group, and by keeping our obedience for our relationship to grow. He will never fill the void if we keep ignoring Him.

God wants you to be interested in Him, and then He will reveal Himself to you. In Psalm 37:4 it says, "Delight yourself also in the LORD, and He shall give you the desires of your heart." God, the Creator of gold and diamonds and the world wants, to have a close relationship with you. He wants to look after you and help you live a life worth living.

However, many would still hesitate, doubt, or think twice on the reality or validity of this relationship. Why? Because more than likely, they do not want anybody like God to tell them what to do. Just like Satan, they want to be gods instead of letting God be the boss of their lives. Some will allow their manager at work or their spouse to be the boss of their life, but they will not let God, who gives them everything, to be the manager of their life. A soldier, for instance, would want to be a sergeant instead of letting the sergeant teach him how to become a soldier. They are like rebellious kids thinking that they know better than their parents. Not allowing God to be the boss of your life is meaningless, and you should know it by now. God made you for a purpose, and if you find that purpose, you will find the meaning of life.

Jesus said, "If you cling to your life, you will lose it; but if you give it up for me, you will find it (Matthew 10:39)." Jesus says it again after several chapters, "If you try to keep your life for yourself, you will lose it. But, if you give up your life for me, you will find true life. (Matthew 16:25). Draw near to God, and He will draw near to you. Two of my Christian favorite songs say something like this in the lyrics, "I'd rather have Jesus than silver and gold" and "You are worth more than diamonds." Why do you think that the writer of these songs prefers Jesus than diamonds or gold? In my opinion, it is because these things are just rocks. God is worth more than rocks because He not only created these stones but the universe as well. Likewise, God values you more than any precious jewels, and He is more interested in you and in who you are than your wealth. God loves you so much He wants to be a part of your life.

> Such a relationship with our Creator is *the key* to abundant living, for there is no greater, more satisfying accomplishment than that among men! When we reach this point, we will have learned the godly perspective, and we will know that the life of God we live is definitely abundant living—

no matter what our circumstance (Philippians 4:11)![11]

Having a loving relationship with God surpasses human understanding since it is the very source of life. It is an awesome relationship because it is sustained by God. In one of my readings, I came across this passage, "Real life is given and sustained by God. To deny God is to embrace death. To assert a life independent from God is to repeat Adam and Eve's attempt to be like God. Now, as then, it brings decay and death."

Life with Christ is abundant because it is sustained by the Creator Himself. Christ becomes our spiritual nourishment. Jesus said, "I am the bread of life. He who comes to me will never go hungry, and he who believes in me will never be thirsty" (John 6:35). A personal relationship with Christ is the greatest gift that a person will ever receive.

Relationship with Mankind

Life is even more wonderful if we love God and if we are at peace with our family, relatives, friends, and the people around us. This life is fulfilling, has meaning, and is worth living. It gives power and strength to life. It gives humanity the reason for existence, and it gives purpose and vitality to living.

Now what was your answer to the question, what is a life that is fulfilling, has meaning, and is worth living? Most of you may have come up with different answers. But to some, the answer would probably still be having a big house, nice car, and lots of money. Now again, the question that I will ask is, are these things meaningful to you? Money, in my opinion, does not give meaning because it is never fulfilling. It is a thing that you always want and need regardless if you are rich or poor or if you have plenty or none. It never satisfies. But nevertheless, is having money more fulfilling than having a good, loving, happy, relationship with your husband, children, or friends and relatives?

Now think about it deeply. We have been greatly deceived in believing that an abundant life is having wealth. What is wealth if you are living by yourself in a mansion but have no one to laugh with or to share your deepest thoughts or feelings? What is wealth if you barely talk to your wife or your children? What is wealth if your health is going down the drain because you neglected it while trying to accumulate wealth? What is more important, having a lot of money or being with someone you love and enjoying peace of mind, serenity, happiness, and well-being?

I was in Canada in 2007 when a devastating fire in Southern California happened. It was known to be the most devastating fire in that area that the people have ever seen. I was glued to the television since I have relatives who live near the fire location in San Diego. I was also watching the reactions of the people who have lost their homes. Almost everyone was glad that their family is safe. It is comforting to know that most of them valued their family more than their belongings. Some brought their extended families—their cats and dogs that they loved—instead of their expensive personal belongings to the shelters. Most of them were more concerned with their family's well-being than their possessions. Most knew that they could rebuild their homes later, and knowing that their families were safe and intact was the most important thing. It was evident that they valued their relationships more than their properties.

Meaningful relationships should be valued more than money or wealth. It is the correct philosophy of life. It should be esteemed more than anything since it is the purpose of our existence. A marriage, for instance, that is full of trust, love, respect, and encouragement and that grows deeper and more meaningful as years go by is invaluable. There is no price value for this relationship. Relationships is where we can make a positive impact on others' lives. We can influence and change others' perspectives and lives. I hope the point I am trying to get across is clear. Meaningful and abundant relationship should be valued more than anything, more than money or gold. After all, it is the real and true meaning of life.

Having a good relationship with God and men is what makes life abundant and meaningful. Many wealthy people try to buy happiness, but you and I know that it seldom works. Anybody can have a happy and meaningful life because it is not for sale, but it takes work and right choices. Like trees, relationships need nurturing and tender love and care. Some of us are never taught, trained, or educated to achieve a successful relationship. But with a little guidance, like the ones we already outlined, we can achieve healthy, meaningful relationships with God and men.

CHAPTER 13

ABUNDANT LIVING AND TRUTH

Abundant life means understanding the meaning of life, but it also involves honesty and truthfulness. Truth is important because it can build or break relationships. It sometimes makes an enemy a friend and a friend an enemy. It is also a word and an action that is difficult to do, to handle, or to define. But regardless of how we define *truth*, to some, it is not good enough; there is no ending to it, especially when one thinks that there is no truth or truth could be relative. Even the philosophers have been trying to debate truth for centuries. Regardless, truth here is not a lie, and it is a reality or actuality of a situation or a thing. It is another element that adds meaning to abundant life.

Life is more meaningful if what you learn, what you say, what you think, and what you do is true. If your line of work, for instance, is selling drugs, then your job is dangerous and heartless because it ruins instead of build lives. Your work must make a positive difference in order for your work to be meaningful. If you think of things that are impure, then stop because your immoral thoughts could lead to unhealthy desires leading to sin. These unhealthy thoughts do not add value to your life. It will, in fact, more than likely ruin your good life. If you say things that are not true and can hurt someone, then what you say is not significant. You know that what you say is meaningful if it makes a positive influence. If you are just gossiping, you are not making a significant difference. There is no self-satisfaction in doing or saying things that are not true.

Nowadays some people are afraid to do and say the right things because they are afraid to suffer the consequences. Some are reluctant to reveal the truth because they don't want to be embarrassed or to get in trouble. Some do not want to mention the truth against their boss at work because they are afraid that they may lose their or their friend's jobs.

But truth should not be a matter of offense but a matter for defense. People should not be afraid to do or say the right thing since most of the time, it has its way of eventually manifesting, and the consequence is usually graver than we expect. Truth will prevail even if it is corroborated to be false. We all know many true stories of people who stood for the truth who became heroes, like Martin Luther King Jr. and Eric Liddell in the *Chariots of Fire* movie. In their case, speaking the truth had satisfying rewards. They were persecuted and hindered for doing the right things, but they did it anyway, and the end result was admirable. People should not be fearful to do the right thing, especially if we do it at the right time in an appropriate manner. But even if we are cursed for doing the right things, in the end, the result is a blessing. God and men will honor you more if you are truthful.

Accepting criticisms that are true are blessings as well. Nowadays, many do not want to tell the truth because it may be perceived as an offense and often lead to hurt feelings or worse. But graciously accepting the truth or criticism is a good thing and sometimes godsend. How are we going to know what we do wrong if no one tells us? If someone tells us that we gossip too much, that should be taken as a warning or a correction. It should tell us that we are not doing something right and we need to change our ways. Changing ourselves from the negative to positive is good, and if someone is pointing our negative, it is good. It is sometimes hard for people to sugarcoat the sinful things that we do. So we should be understanding, accepting and should commit to change and move on. Instead of being offended or hurt, we should be thankful to the person who pointed it out, whether it is true or untrue. If it is untrue, be gracious anyways. You will impart a blessing to the person criticizing you.

I was listening to a radio on my way home one day, and the guest was saying, "My boss told me quite a while back that I will never get promoted. So I told him, 'Thank you for telling me that, and I admire your openness. Some people hesitate and do not have that courage to say that.' What he said did not bother me because I know who I am—I am a child of God. Today, that person is under me, and he was never promoted."

It has been said that a man's most prized possession is integrity. A person who loves the truth is smart, understanding, and is safe from confrontation and judgement. Truth keeps our conscience free from radicals, and it keeps us from torment. Abundant life is learning, talking, and breathing the truth. It is the application of truth that makes life more challenging and profoundly meaningful.

CHAPTER 14

ABUNDANT LIFE AND LEARNING

Another important element in human living that makes life more abundant is the joy of learning. God is the source of all knowledge, and He has granted us with powerful brains so we can increase our life and perpetuate ourselves to greater abundance. As mentioned earlier, He gave humans unique and powerful brains that have the ability to process things, such as computing, analyzing, interpreting, organizing, perceiving, and imagining things. It has the capability to store memories and information as well as create things. God gave us this type of brain because there is joy, pleasure, and meaning in learning something. He has blessed humans with enduring hunger for knowledge so we can fulfill a purpose or so we can learn about something that we are passionate about. Learning enhances a person's life and others. By learning how to be a doctor, we increase our self-worth, the quality of our living, and we can help others too. More often than not, it makes a person feel great, whether it's learning how to play a guitar or how to build a spaceship. Humans should not cease from learning. It is one of the greatest gifts that our loving Creator endowed humanity to make his or her life count, to make it more interesting, challenging, and profoundly meaningful.

Learning does not only improve ourselves, but it also brings joy, pleasure, excitement, and fulfillment. Learning is a privilege and a gift. It is a privilege to be a pilot, to be an engineer, philosopher, doctor, or a cook. It is fulfilling to be a doctor, a scientist, or a governor. I once had a poor co-worker who said, "If only I could fly an airplane, I could die happy." This person could have probably been the best pilot on earth if only he was given the opportunity to become one.

Children are the happiest people on earth because they do not cease to learn. But once they become adults and stop learning, some become stagnant, boring, and unproductive. I have a notebook that has this quote on the cover that says, "Learning is like rowing upstream. Not to advance is to drop back." Thomas Jefferson, the third president of the United States, said, "A mind always employed is always happy. This is true secret, the grand recipe for felicity."

But to some of us, where did the joy of learning go? Why do some people cease to learn at a certain point? Was it because of lack of money, motivation, or discouragement? My joy of wanting to learn the piano when I was a child went away because we were poor, and we could not afford the cost of a piano lesson. My co-worker's desire to be a pilot became just a dream because of merely being poor as well. He could not afford the cost of a university degree. My best friend's joy of wanting to be an astronaut went away because he had poor eyesight. He was told that to be an astronaut one must have a pair of good eyes. My other friend lost her joy of learning because she simply did not have the time to study. Unfortunately, most of us have lost the joy of acquiring knowledge due to unfortunate circumstances. But fortunately, our loving God opens up other opportunities for joy, for us to continue to learn whether young or old. He usually stirs up dreams that had long been forgotten or fan the flame of learning. I have lost the desire to learn piano and my best friend is now too old to become an astronaut, but we both found new joy in doing and learning other things. My best friend is pursuing his PhD, and I am finding my joy in learning foreign languages.

Someone once said knowledge is power. This is true in almost all cases since the world has reached the moon because of knowledge. We have developed advanced technologies because of inspired individuals. Learning advances not only one's self or others but the world as well. Some of the greatest persons who made impacts to the world know three or four languages, can play a musical instrument, and have at least one degree. Some of the popes, royalties, and politicians are usually trained in this way. Some are highly educated because it is expected of them and they can afford it. But some should have acquired knowledge because of the mere joy of learning and because of the fulfillment and the skill, competence, power, and the positive influence that it contributes to the world.

Life is even more fulfilling if what one learns makes a positive contribution or is relevant in changing our life or someone else's life. If you are a politician, for instance, and you make laws to protect the innocent, then you have revolutionized the world to a new and better direction. But if as a politician you haven't done anything significant, then your life and the life of others, including history, is stagnant. As a politician, you haven't done any positive thing that is worth writing in the history books. Your career as a politician will be more fulfilling if you further the needs of the needy and not your own hidden deceptive agenda. Martin Luther King Jr. changed history by working on eliminating racism. As a result of his noble intention, there is now a street named after him and a holiday dedicated to celebrate and commemorate his admirable and successful intent. By his knowledge and his passionate desire to live the God-given truth, he changed history. True knowledge has power, and when this knowledge is used to change the evil for good, it is even more powerful. King Jr. has revolutionized the world and the kingdom of God because now we see black, brown, or white, rich or poor, living and worshipping Christ together.

God said, "My people are destroyed for lack of knowledge" (Hosea 4:6). As mentioned earlier, politicians and the media are very good at convincing their audience that what they say is true. The question is, do you know for certain that what they are telling you is true? Are you knowledgeable, learned, or informed enough to know that what they say is accurate? Do you have good logical and analytical skills that could decipher their motives? History revealed that Hitler lied and used the Jews as a scapegoat to fulfill his hidden agenda of wanting to rule the world. He deceived and killed millions, and he could have deceived you as well. Many were blinded from the truth. He is one example of a politician who speaks of goodwill, but his motives are for destruction. Do you know for certain that the candidate you are voting for office has the right motives? Or are you one of those that are deceived because of lack of knowledge?

Understanding the wisdom that learning contributes to life is invaluable to our existence. One's success is often based on his or her application of learning. When we continue to learn, we continue to grow in wisdom, in knowledge, and in truth. God gives us this purpose to keep us on our toes and to give us the opportunity to be productive. Knowledge delivers humans from ignorance, and it is through education that we improve our life—we develop self-esteem, strength, power, and we maximize our potential. It allows us to grow and to discern what's reality and what's not, what truth is compared to deception. It is in knowing the truth that we can fight oppressive leaders and any form of injustice. It is in learning and living the truth that our society stands, and it is through knowledge that we become bold and we are able to rise above.

We are blessed with brains that allow for the opportunity to learn and to make a positive impact in this world. We were placed here to be a better person and not worse, to make a better place and not make it worse. Through learning, our potential is limitless, our life is abundant, and we can change this world into a brighter tomorrow.

CONCLUSION

Life on earth is abundant, but some are not experiencing this kind of life because they have a wrong perspective on life. Almost everyone aspires to be wealthy, whether we are rich or poor, and we do not want to admit it, but some would even cheat, lie, and kill for money. To most, money is the solution to all problems. Some, without even realizing, destroy the lives of the very ones they love and the life of others in the process of accumulating for their own self-interests. Some have focused on building treasures here on earth instead of building treasures in heaven.

The Creator of life did not promise us a big house, luxurious car, expensive jewelry, or enormous wealth; He promised us abundant life. And He continues to offer the secret of abundant life every day regardless of our economic status. Abundant life emanates from realizing that the material wealth we have is not the means of abundant life. One thing is for sure, we are not going to take it with us when we die. What is ours that we take with us is our spirit, our soul, our essence, our being, or what we are inside our heart. What's important is what we have done that have impacted someone in a positive way. What we do with the relationships that we are privileged to have is more important than money or gold. What we have are just instruments for living; they are not life. So value the relationships that you are privileged to have, whether it's your children, your parents, your brothers and sisters, or your spouse. More importantly, value your relationship with your Creator.

Abundant life is realizing that the most valuable gift in this world is God's presence in your life. Growth through Christ is essential to experiencing an abundant life because He wants to clean us from impurities that we accumulate every day. He wants our life to count, to be worthy, and to be abundant. Life without Christ often falls short of the true happiness that we all seek. The presence of God in our life is the presence of love and genuine righteousness. The fun of living comes when we are guided by God's hand, and consequently, we could do more with our lives than we could ever do on our own.

We are precious to God—that's why He longs for everyone to have abundant life, that's why He created the earth that's full of blessings. His magnificent creation illustrates His existence and to show His great love for you and me. He even sent Christ to redeem us from hell, to show us how to live, and to reveal his nature. In addition, He sent his Holy Spirit as his voice for those who are willing to listen. But unfortunately, to the biased mind, tens of thousands of marvelous designs cannot prove a designer. The biased mind denies the existence of God, rejects the Holy Spirit, and hence misses out on abundant life.

If you do not believe in God, or let's say there is no God, then what you do in this lifetime may matter, but you will never fulfill your life's purpose that God intended. If there is a God, then you would miss out on the abundant life that Christ offered here on earth and through eternity. You will miss out not only on God's tender love, mercy, and joy but also on the opportunity to go to heaven someday.

Life could be a beautiful painting or a musical masterpiece. Each person has the capability to create, write, author, or paint his or her own masterpiece. Implementing the elements of right living that was discussed, such as growing spiritually, building treasures in heaven, understanding the value of relationships, contentment, health, and learning are necessary to experiencing an abundant life. Sometimes it may not be perfect, but it is meaningful and fulfilling. It is a masterpiece not only in our own way, but in others, especially those who are close to us. But more importantly, it is a masterpiece to God.

Life is abundant if what we do in this life is abundant. It is abundant if we are growing spiritually, if we are enriching our lives with knowledge, truth, love, wisdom, and understanding. It is abundant if we live in the guidance of God's love, if we pursue righteousness instead of sinfulness, if we pursue love instead of hatred, if we build relationships instead of ruining them, if we build treasures in heaven instead of wealth here on earth. There is a sense of peace and fulfillment when we die if we live the God-given purpose of our lives. By correctly implementing the elements of right living and by allowing God to guide our hands to compose a beautiful masterpiece that stirs the heart, the angels will sing "Hallelujah!"

NOTES

[1] Emil Brunner and Karl Barth, *Natural Theology: Comprising "Nature and Grace" by Professor Dr. Emil Brunner and the reply "No!" by Dr. Karl Barth* (Eugene: Wipf and Stock Publishers, 2002), page 24.

[2] Shawn Dorman, *Inside a U.S. Embassy: How the Foreign Service Works for America* (American Foreign Service Association, 2003), page 102.

[3] Bonaventure, *The Journey of the Mind to God*, trans. Philotheus Boehner, ed. with introduction and notes Stephen F. Brown (Hackett Publishing Company, 1993), 10.

[4] Richard T. Ritenbaugh, "Are You Living the Abundant Life?," *Forerunner*, July 2005, 8, https://pdf.cgg.org/4rnr1406.pdf, page 23.

[5] Brunner and Barth, *Natural Theology*, xx

[6] Ritenbaugh, "Are You Living," 7.

[7] "Education News, Schools, Colleges, Higher Education, Technical Education," The Hindu, last modified July 13, 2002, https://www.hindu.com/thehindu/quest/200207/stories/2002071301530200.html.

[8] "John Balguy Quote," A-Z Quotes, https://www.azquotes.com/quote/661768.

[9] "Swami Sivananda Quotes," BrainyQuote, https://www.brainyquote.com/quotes/swami_sivananda_155121.

[10] "Mahatma Gandhi Quotes," BrainyQuote, https://www.brainyquote.com/quotes/mahatma_gandhi_160874.

[11] Ritenbaugh, "Are You Living," 14.

ABOUT THE AUTHOR

M. Smith is a mother, a wife, and a state employee, who has traveled to many countries and has lived in the Philippines, Canada, Europe, and the United States. She has a degree in business administration with a major in international business. She became a Christian in 1992 and has walked with the Lord on a special journey ever since. This book is an account of what she learned walking with the Lord over many years.